QUILTING

FOR PEOPLE WHO DON'T HAVE TIME TO QUILT!

BOOK ONE: Sew-Before-You-Cut Patchwork

"Let's start with strips and squares"

Featuring:

- A Have Fun Attitude
- Basic Machine Quilting
- Self-teaching Step by Step Projects
- Precision Patchwork Without Patterns

By Marti Michell

 Published by American School of Needlework, Inc., ASN Publishing, 1455 Linda Vista Drive, San Marcos, CA 92069

ISBN: 0-88195-187-0 Printed in U.S.A. 14 15 16 17 18 19

Before You Begin

If you are thinking "I just don't have time to make quilts", stop right there, wipe your mental slate clean and get ready for fun. The "Quilting for People Who Don't Have Time to Quilt" techniques presented in this book will show you how to **enjoy making** quilts for people to **enjoy using!**

Quilts are a universal symbol of love and warmth. For centuries, men and women alike, have been
  protected by quilts,
  intrigued with their history,
  inspired by their beauty,
  and fascinated with the process of making quilts.

The antique quilts we enjoy today are indeed slices of history. We examine them carefully. We look at quilts for clues about the maker's life. We see a quilt and remember a Grandmother or our own childhood events fondly. Most of us try to preserve and protect these heirlooms. Sometimes we forget that quilts were originally made to be used. For every quilt existing today perhaps dozens more were made and used. Think how much love and comfort those quiltmakers provided.

With electric blankets and central heat, no one quilts because they need to be warm. So why do people quilt today? There is no single reason, but here are a few of the answers.

"to satisfy my creative urges"
"for relaxation"
"I love working with fabrics"
"to leave something of myself"
"for gifts"
"to use up fabric"
"it's infectious, I can't quit"
"as a showcase for my needlework"
"to make a scrapbook or memory quilt"
"to express my love and provide comfort for my family and friends"
"I've just always wanted to make a quilt"

Perhaps you've made that last comment and this book is intended to help you have the opportunity to make a quilt.

EMPHASIS IS ON QUILTS TO USE

While I emphasize making quilts to **use**, these techniques are so accurate and so productive that you can incorporate them into "heirloom" and competitive quilting, too. You know what heirloom quilts are don't you? Quilts that are too good for your family to use, but not too good for an heir to use or some complete stranger to take to the beach in a hundred years.

One of the fabulous by-products of making quilts with these techniques and attitudes is that you make quilts to satisfy yourself. You aren't making quilts to please me or your mother-in-law or a quilt show judge or a snooty sister. Instead, you can make quilts that you like, that express your own creative urges, make a statement or tell a joke. You can use the quilt or give it to someone—no strings attached.

Imagine it. You've worked on the "heirloom" quilt for five years when your son, your first born, announces he's getting married. Then the big decision. You'll give them THE quilt for a wedding present.

What do you think happens on your first visit? The thing you want to see first is the quilt. You are discreetly looking and suddenly you see it. "Oh no! Is that cat on **my** quilt?!?" They can't please you. You'll be mad if they don't use it and mad if they do!

When you sit down to make an "heirloom", every decision becomes momentous. I prefer the relaxed attitude I call automatic heirlooms. My recommendation is to flood your family with quilts. Make so many they can't use them all up. Then there will be plenty for future generations.

We will be making quilts that can be finished in hours, not months or years. Our techniques include multiple cutting, machine piecing and machine quilting. You will be learning to make specific quilts, but more importantly, you will learn methods that you can adapt to many different quilts.

I don't like using the words easy or fast or quick because too many people turn up their noses and say "Humph—

that means big pieces, sloppy workmanship, low standards." No-No-No! Every technique introduced here is easier, faster and more accurate than what could be called traditional techniques.

What about masterpiece quilts? You may want to make quilts that are "too good to use", the kind that only sit on a shelf in an acid free box to be brought down on momentous occasions. Or you may decide competition quilting is your goal. That's fine. These techniques will allow you to make those quilts more quickly and accurately, too.

THINK POSITIVELY

Start by forgetting everything you ever knew or assumed about cutting hundreds of separate pieces and sewing them back together one by one. You are going to learn how to sew many pieces together **before** cutting. A clue, everything you can sew before you cut is more accurate, faster and easier.

Let's get rid of the #1 myth about quilt making. It's the "I could never do that" syndrome. Many people look at quilts like they are all monumental, never ending projects. Probably because we all know at least one person who has been working on the same quilt for 30 years. The truth is, that person hasn't really worked on the quilt for 30 years; they just haven't finished the quilt for 30 years.

MAKE QUALITY QUILTS QUICKLY

You can make quality quilts quickly. You do have to follow my simple rules.

Rule #1: You must be selective.

It is important to understand that every quilt you've ever seen can not be made using these techniques. You'll notice no curved seams or complicated pointed designs. There are, however, more quilts that can be made this way than anyone will live long enough to accomplish.

In this book all of the designs are made from strips. That doesn't mean that everything in the finished quilt is a strip. It just means that the first cut on every piece is a strip.

Rule #2: You must be selective.

You always pick out the pattern and fabrics for every quilt. You never agree or offer to make a quilt for anyone if they want to pick the design and fabrics. This may sound rude, but if they want to do the picking, they do the piecing. If you get to pick, you'll piece. (You'll understand this better if you ever weaken and agree to make a quilt someone else selected.)

Warning: Once you even say you're thinking about making a quilt, someone you care about a lot will say, "Oh, will you make one for me?" Remember if you say "Yes", add "as long as I get to make all the decisions".

YOU'LL LEARN TO THINK GRIDS

Patchwork is the procedure of sewing small pieces of different fabrics, usually cut in geometric shapes, together in pleasing patterns. Applique is the process of applying cut fabric shapes (usually not geometric) directly onto another layer of fabric. We will be making patchwork quilt tops.

The most frequently used shapes in patchwork are squares, right angle triangles and strips. This book will deal with strips and squares. There are no pattern pieces. Any quilt that can be drawn on a grid (like graph paper) can be made with these techniques. If it can be drawn on a grid, you can decide on any size and are not confined to fixed pattern pieces. The size of the first strip you cut determines the scale and finished size of the project.

In A Nutshell

One of the best things about quilting is there are very few rights or wrongs, mostly opinions. Many of the following sections include boxed IN A NUTSHELL summaries. If you don't want to read the backup information, just skip on to the next NUTSHELL.

What About Fabrics?

There are a few things I feel duty bound to say about fabric selection and preparation. The nutshell synopsis is I like to use 100% cotton fabrics that have been tested for shrinkage and fading. I cut my strips on the lengthwise grain. I cut and never tear. I like to think of my fabric selections as spirited, pretty, surprising or even off-the-wall (if that is the statement I want to make), but not dull or boring which is different from comfortable or safe. The reasons follow.

IS IT TRUE WHAT THEY SAY ABOUT 100% COTTON?

If cotton was King in "the old days", polyester was Queen from the late 1950's through the early 1970's. When I met an elderly Georgia mountain lady and quilter in 1970, I admit I originally considered her demand for 100% cotton an unsophisticated old wives' tale. Armed with my Home Economics degree and a lifetime of sewing, I felt very knowledgeable about fibers. At that time 100% cotton was barely available. It was not recognized as a suitable fiber for women's clothing. I couldn't even remember sewing on 100% cotton. As a quilter, however, I developed a new appreciation for 100% cotton. Here are some of the reasons:

1. COTTON HELPS PREVENT DISTORTION. In the process of sewing many small pieces together, suddenly—for some unknown reason—the carefully cut shapes aren't matching. The seam allowance is perfect. What can it be? Nine times out of ten, you've chosen incompatible fabrics. Usually, the culprit fabric is a blend. Sometimes, it's just a different finish or weight, but incompatible fabrics almost always result in distortion. This means the finished work isn't true, there is puffiness in places, and seams that are supposed to match, don't. This doesn't always happen, just often. Once, when I was trying to make a visual aid of a distorted block using incompatible fabrics, they simply wouldn't distort!

2. COTTON HOLDS A PRESS OR CREASE. When turning under the edge of a fabric for hand applique, a blend pops right back to it's original position and is very difficult to press flat. The edges of a cotton applique "roll" permanently and more easily.

3. COTTON SEEMS TO REDUCE THE RISK OF BATTING "BEARDING" OR FIBER MIGRATION. If the batting you use has a tendency to have little fibers coming through the fabric, the problem is much more prevalent with blends than with 100% cotton.

4. COTTON HAS BETTER "GIVE AND TAKE". This may be saying it distorts less in a different way, but I don't think so.

There is a difference between a fabric helping you through problems and causing them. In this case, I'm saying that using 100% cotton often helps you through problems because a good steam pressing can remove a puckered area and make a puffy piece flat.

5. COTTON IS MORE COMFORTABLE.

6. COTTON IS EASIER TO HAND QUILT. Most hand quilters agree that 100% cotton is easier to "needle" than a blend. The larger the item you're quilting, the more important this is. Several hours a day quilting on a quilt with a blend backing becomes very noticeable in sensitive finger joints.

All of this is not to say you **must** use 100% cotton. It's just to say you should understand the possible problems if you don't. Generally, the more similar the fabrics are in weight and feel, the less the problem. 100% cotton is available today in a fabulous assortment of prints and solids. If you are a beginner, it will be easier if you start by limiting yourself to 100% cotton.

If you must mix fabrics, and you get rippled seams, there are a few tricks to try. If spray sizing is ironed onto the blend, the crisper finish seems to help control the fabric. Tear away background stabilizer (a nonwoven material usually sold where interfacings are sold), placed beneath the fabrics being sewn, may help control the stitching and prevent distortion.

MORE ABOUT FABRIC SELECTION

You're making quilts to express yourself, to satisfy your own creative urges, to make a statement or tell a joke. Select the fabric accordingly. Variety is not only the spice of life, it makes quilts more interesting. A nutshell approach to fabric selection is to look for variety in the fabrics you are combining in a quilt. Not just variety in the colors, but in the scale of the prints, the type of prints, the density, etc. Most importantly, remember that the fabrics selected do more to set the mood of the quilt than the pattern. Consider photo of the two No-Name Four Patch quilts on page 23. The peach and turquoise fabrics are more soft and romantic than the red and white, no matter what style quilt you make.

Here are a few other fabric selection tips.

1. IT IS EASY TO BE BORING. Most beginners tend to be very "matchy-uppy". Unsure of putting several different fabrics together, they will examine fabrics with a magnifying glass to make sure the blues match. Often the result is that when you step back a few feet from the finished item, the fabrics just blend together and look like a printed piece of patchwork.

2. BEING HAPPY WITH YOUR QUILT IS MOST IMPORTANT. Because so many people express a desire to learn more about combining fabrics and color, most of the projects give pointers to help you stretch your fabric imagination.

3. CONSIDER COLOR. If you are making a quilt for a particular room, that color scheme will influence your thoughts. I encourage quilters to feel free about the fabrics they use and let the choices be right for the quilt, not the room. Typically, what's good for the quilt is good for the room.

4. THE APPEARANCE OF TEXTURE IN FABRICS SHOULD NOT BE OVERLOOKED OR UNDERRATED. Generally monochromatic or low contrast small prints just add texture. I often use them instead of solids. From a distance, the quilt has a softer more muted look. Close up, a texture print does not demand fancy quilting. In fact, if you are planning lots of fancy hand quilting, avoid texture prints as they don't do the quilting justice. Conversely, solids can look very empty without lots of hand quilting. You'll notice that I basically use solids as accents.

5. LARGER PRINTS ARE NOT A NO-NO! When you cut a large print into smaller pieces, the images are often completely lost, only the colors and some random shapes remain. So if the colors are just perfect in a large jungle print with 10" elephants, you can probably make a Double Irish Chain without a trace of a trunk!

6. STRIPES NEED SPECIAL CONSIDERATION. The strong directional effect of stripes demands that special attention be given to their cutting and placement in patchwork. When well done the illusions of motion and action can be spectacular.

7. RANDOM DESIGNS MINIMIZE DIRECTIONAL PROBLEMS.

Don't forget to stand back and look at the fabrics before you finalize your selection. If you can't stand back, squint to get the feeling of distance. The appearance of the finished item will be much more important from a distance.

HOW MUCH FABRIC TO BUY

My policy has always been as much as I could afford!

There is, of course, not one answer for how much fabric to make a quilt. All of my estimates used in this book are based on 45"-wide fabrics. Some rules of thumb: Just the backing for a queen/double is 6½ yds so if you add fabric for all those seams and some latitude in cutting I say you need a total of 10 yds for the surface of a not too complicated queen/double quilt. Following the same line of thought, a total of 12½ yds for a king size and 6½ yds for a twin. Crib quilts and wall hangings are in the 2 to 3½ yd amounts.

If you get very serious about quilting, you will probably start collecting fabrics. Or perhaps you are thinking about quilting because you have already collected. Being an experienced speculative fabric buyer myself, let me pass on my three favorite amounts to purchase.

27" is the least I ask someone to cut from the bolt. Almost everything I do starts with a strip and because I cut my strips on the lengthwise grain whenever possible, a quarter yard (9" by 45") just doesn't mean anything. I will buy "fat quarters" that strike my fancy. A fat quarter is a pre-cut piece of fabric 18" by 22½" that many quilt stores feature. They are wonderful if you are collecting as many different pinks as possible", you're in a hurry, or you just want a small piece. As a bonus, the dimension of a fat quarter is a much more useable piece of fabric. You can make a pillow back or a vest section for example.

3½ yds is the amount I buy if it is a fabric I think could ever be used in the border of a quilt. That is the most I would need to cut a king size border with mitered corners on the lengthwise grain. (2½ yds is enough if you are not mitering the corners.) As you use it, you must remember to cut other pieces down one side and leave a long wide piece for borders.

6½ yds is the quantity for something I think is destined to be a backing. However, I've been doing more pieced backs recently, and this is a less frequent speculative purchase.

Don't panic or quit if you run out of fabric for a particular plan. It was probably getting boring anyway. Look at it as an opportunity to be creative in quilt making and problem solving. The real point is to relax about "just the right amount." With so many variables, expecting to come out even is not realistic. A little extra is always nice for accessories.

WHAT SIZE IS A QUILT?

How much fabric you need to buy is really a function of what size quilt you are making. Quilts are used so many ways that another way to look at it is running out of fabric can determine the size of your quilt. When you make quilts for fun, that is, just because you want to, they can be any size.

Size is only crucial when you are making a quilt for a specific bed. Even then, personal choices enter into size. Do you want it to hang to the floor or just skim a dust ruffle? Do you like a deep pillow tuck with huge pillows or will your quilt go under pillows? The best way to determine size is to put a large bed sheet on the chosen bed so that it hangs down and tucks and covers as you like. Measure and add 2″-4″ in both directions for the amount that the quilting takes up. This is your optimum size. Be aware that as you get into planning quilts for specific sizes compromises often have to be made. A 12″ block doesn't always fit the perfect number of times in both directions, leaving an equal amount for borders all around.

When I can't measure the bed, I use these quilt size guidelines. Except for the crib size, they were developed by adding a 9″ pillow tuck and a 13″ drop to three sides of standard mattress sizes.

Crib—Small 30″ x 45″; large 40″ x 60″
Twin—65″ x 97″
Double—80″ x 97″
Queen—86″ x 102″; Queen/Double 84″ x 100″
King—104″ x 102″

TO TEAR OR TO CUT?

I cut.

Most fabric stores do one or the other and I accept their choice. My understanding is that before easy-care finishes, we tore. Then the next step was pulling on opposite ends to "straighten". With easy care finishes, when you tear, there is often distortion in the fabric as much as an inch in both directions. After you tear fabric with an easy-care finish, you can wash it and pull it and press it and convince yourself that you've straightened the goods. The next time you wash them, however, they will distort back to the original position. So, as a matter of preference, I cut fabric and accept the fact that "what you see is what you get".

TO PREWASH OR NOT TO PREWASH?

It's so easy to say prewash all your fabrics and just be done with it, but I don't do it or say it. I do **pretest** all fabrics as I select them for a particular project.

There are lots of reasons why I don't automatically wash everything. The colors and finish are more appealing to me before they are washed. I like the feel of the fabric better before washing. Rationalization or not, I think the crispness of unwashed fabrics is easier to work with using machine techniques. Some people who only hand quilt have told me they think prewashed fabric needles more easily. Besides, my acquired amount of fabric would have taken a considerable time to wash. It also stacks better straight from the bag.

One of the interesting things to me is that as an antique quilt collector, I have observed that there are two things people find especially charming about antique quilts. One is the quilt or top that "has never been washed". The other is the quilt that has an almost puckered look because it shrank evenly and considerably when washed. Prewashing fabrics was not a historic thing to do. I pick my traditions carefully and if "they" didn't prewash fabrics, I don't need to either.

How to test
I cut 2″ x 12″ strips of each fabric for the project. I hold them under very hot water. If the color is going to run, you see it right there. Most bleeding is excess dye—that is, the dye is "spent" and will not permanently color another fabric, only the water, but you still need to deal with the fabric. Washing to get out the excess dye is the safest. Then test again.

Usually, no color runs. When the strips are thoroughly saturated, I squeeze out the excess water and iron the strips dry. If they are going to shrink, they will do it then. It is the heat on the wet fiber that causes shrinkage. Then I compare the strips. If they have shrunk evenly and minimally, I still don't prewash. I do prewash if there is an unusual shrinker. Industry standards allow 2-3% shrinkage, or about $\frac{1}{4}$″ in a 12″ strip.

How to prewash
When I do need to prewash for shrinking, I don't wash the fabric with detergent and triple rinses. That just excessively damages the finish and the color. I find it effective to put the fabric in an automatic washer with warm water, agitate for a few minutes to make sure the fabric is saturated, and spin dry. Then dry it in the dryer but don't over dry. Electric dryers are especially guilty of over drying.

SUN TESTING

Everyone is allowed to work on at least one "masterpiece" quilt. I would sun test fabrics for that or for a wall hanging. One fabric that fades unusually quickly will change the effect of the work. Sometimes Mother Nature is smarter, but it won't be what you had planned. Just put samples of the desired fabrics in your sunniest window. After three days of strong sun, compare to the original fabric. If there are some changes, but not major, I would leave the fabrics another week to see if there is further deterioration.

Terms to Know

Life will be easier if you are in control of geometric terms.
Parallel—lines extending in the same direction at the same distance apart so as to never meet.
Perpendicular—a straight line at right angles to another straight line.
Right Angle—an angle of 90 degrees—sometimes called a square corner.
Square—a four-sided figure having all its sides equal and all its corners right angles.
Vertical—straight up and down.
Horizontal—parallel to the horizon, perpendicular to vertical, straight across.
Lengthwise—in the same direction as the length.

LEARNING ABOUT GRAINLINE AND HOW TO USE IT TO ADVANTAGE

> Whenever possible put the longest outside dimension of a piece on the lengthwise grain. This includes strips!! I cut them lengthwise if possible.

The best way to study grainline properties of fabric is with a piece of woven (not knit) fabric in your hands. With at least an 18" square, and at least one selvage edge in tact, you can learn to **feel** grainline. Grasp the fabric with both hands on the selvage and approximately 18" apart (**Fig A**, positions 1 and 2). Pull in opposite directions to make fabric taut. That's the **lengthwise grain**. The fabric has very little stretch in that direction, but it does have some stretch.

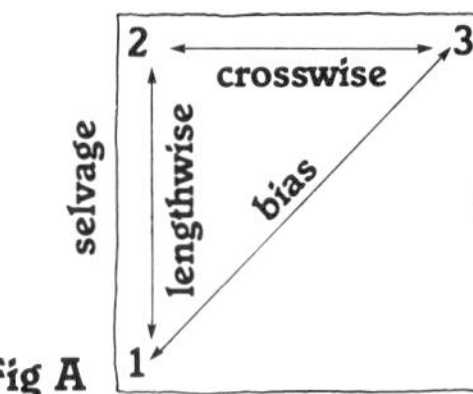

Fig A

Now hold the fabric with one hand on the selvage and the other hand about 18" into the fabric (**Fig A**, positions 2 and 3). Pull again. Isn't that a surprise? That's the **crosswise grain**. It will stretch 2½ to 3 times farther than the lengthwise grain with the same pressure. Most commercial dress patterns suggest placement on lengthwise or crosswise grain. The inference is that they are the same. The fact is that they are not the same.

This is the main reason I stress lengthwise grain on the longest dimension of a piece whenever possible. Lengthwise grain on the long dimension of a border adds a great deal of stability, especially if the item is intended as a wall hanging and has an obvious top. In patchwork being made into garments, whenever possible and when not contrary to the design statement, the lengthwise grain should run from head to toe.

In solid color fabrics, there is often a visible color difference between the lengthwise and crosswise grain—especially visible in larger pieces such as alternate plain blocks.

Another important reason for cutting strips on the lengthwise grain centers around the fabric problem called "bowing". That is when the crosswise threads have been pulled out of position and instead of being perfectly perpendicular to the selvage, they are arched. If you then cut perpendicular strips, you are cutting (breaking) the crosswise threads and everywhere they break, they will ravel. When fabric is bowed, any directional design in the fabric is pulled out of position, too. Cutting crosswise makes that distortion more obvious, **Fig B**.

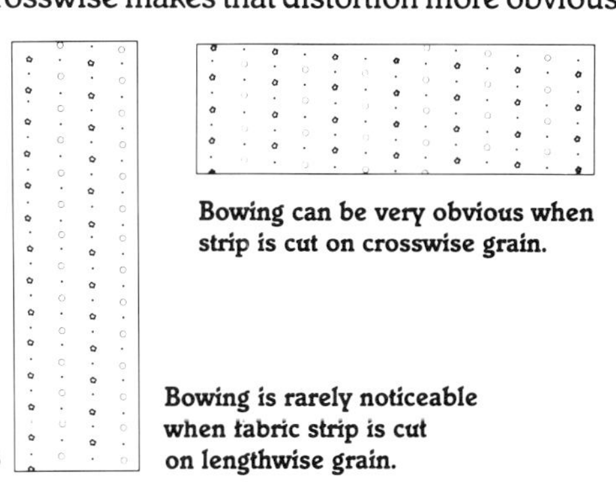

Bowing can be very obvious when strip is cut on crosswise grain.

Bowing is rarely noticeable when fabric strip is cut on lengthwise grain.

Fig B

Bowing barely effects lengthwise grain. Cutting strips on the lengthwise grain keeps printed patterns more accurate and greatly reduces raveling.

The first thing that you do after sewing strips together is to press them. Strips cut on the lengthwise grain do not stretch out of shape as easily as those cut on the crosswise grain. Strips cut crosswise are 45" long. I have adopted 27" (¾ yd) as my standard for lengthwise strips. It is a more comfortable length than 45" to work with, and a reasonable amount to buy. While you lose some of the economies of length, I believe it is justified by the improved quality.

This is not to encourage you to become obsessed with the issue of lengthwise grain. Just try to think ahead, before long, it becomes natural.

There are times when the "trade off" required to use lengthwise grain in the longest dimension isn't worth it—like:

1. OVERRIDING DESIGN DECISION. If the fabric has an obvious directional design that is an integral part of the design and contradicts the lengthwise grain choice—design is more important. Example: printed stripe runs lengthwise. You want the stripe to go crosswise on the border for its dramatic effect. The longest dimension ends up cut with the crosswise grain—go for it!
2. SIMPLE ECONOMICS. You aren't willing to buy 3 to 3½ yards of fabric 45" wide to cut 4 full-size borders on lengthwise grain that will only use 12" of width. That's legitimate. You are the only one that can make that decision. However, since you will have to piece to cut your borders crosswise, why not buy the fabric needed and still cut strips lengthwise and piece. You may end up with more seams on the long side, but I believe it's worth the trade off.
3. IT'S ALREADY SEWN WHEN YOU REMEMBER. Only you can decide when to rip.

What about bias?
Bias isn't a four letter word. Well it is, but it's one you need in your sewing vocabulary and you need to know how to use it! Go back to the 18" square of fabric and put your hands on opposite corners (**Fig A**, positions 1 and 3). Pull. Now that's stretch! There are times when that property will drive you crazy and times when you'll love it. The important thing is to understand bias exists—it is a property of the fabric that does not change—and learn how to work with it. Obviously you do **not** want bias on the longest dimension of a piece. You do **not** want it on a long edge where you might be adding borders next, for example. But if you need flexibility and stretch, like on a narrow rolled binding along a scalloped edge, you'll bless bias.

Space and Tools

WHAT ABOUT YOUR STUDIO?

I highly recommend that you make quilts in the studio. You may physically be working on a folding table in the kitchen, but if you are mentally in "the studio" your results are definitely better.

SEWING MACHINE TIPS

> You really do need a sewing machine to take full advantage of the techniques offered in this series.

Don't panic, you don't need a fancy machine. It must stitch forward. The tension must be properly adjusted. If it isn't, you can get puckered seams (tension too tight) or fabrics actually pull apart and stitches show through on the right side of the seam (tension too loose). 10 to 12 stitches per inch is nice for piecing.

If you haven't used your machine in a while, dust it off, oil it, clean out the lint, put in a new needle [size 14/90] and adjust the tension. Read your owner's manual for help. It doesn't matter that the needle isn't bent, if you can't remember changing it, it's too dull for this work.

Hand piecing can be very enjoyable for people who like handwork, it is almost a necessity for some very intricate piecing, and it can be adapted to these techniques so that it can move along faster. **BUT** if you want the real benefits of the "Quilting for People Who Don't Have Time to Quilt" techniques, piece by machine. Then, we'll even learn how to quilt by machine.

THREADS

Use good quality 100% cotton or cotton wrapped polyester thread for machine piecing. You will use lots of thread, but don't be tempted by cheap thread. In most cases matching colors is not important. You can sometimes find large spools of natural that will save money without compromising quality. It's a good idea to wind at least a half dozen bobbins when you start.

For machine quilting there is a very fine nylon transparent thread that I often prefer to use on the top of my machine with regular sewing machine thread in the bobbin.

Quilting thread is reserved for hand quilting.

THE ROTARY CUTTING SYSTEM

OR Whoever said, "I can't wait to get home and cut!"?

One of the reasons these techniques are so effective is the rotary cutter, a tool introduced in the mid 1970's. Used with a protective mat and acrylic ruler, it speeds you through the cutting process straight to the fun part. Let's face it, cutting can be very tedious, especially if you are looking at a quilt and seeing nearly 1000 squares to cut. Doesn't it sound better to say 100 strips? Or by cutting multiple layers, 25 cuts? More important than fast, is accurate. Accurate cutting is the first crucial step in accurate patchwork. The rotary cutting system is more accurate than traditional methods.

This is stressed so much because I ignored the rotary cutter for several years. After all, I was good with my scissors and I had good scissors. Surely this advanced pizza cutter was just a gadget—right? WRONG! Please don't ignore rotary cutters.

There are several brands available in two sizes. Some people feel more comfortable starting with the smaller cutter. If you want to reduce your investment, it is less expensive. Because I do mostly multiple layer cutting, I prefer the larger cutter.

People say—"How can you use that to cut fabric and not cut your table?" You can't!! That's where the protective mat comes in. You must use the cutter on the mat or your table will look like the bottom of a used pizza pan!

Don't try to substitute. Leftover linoleum doesn't work. Old stacks of newspaper won't work. The self-healing mat designed for the job won't dull the blade like other surfaces might. There are many sizes. As you might suspect, the larger

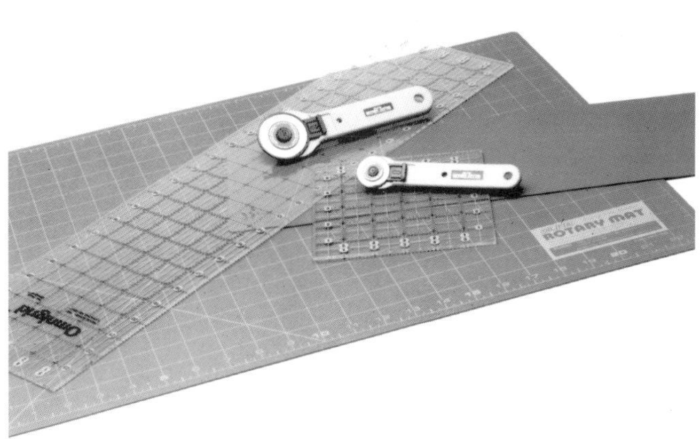

the mat, the more expensive. For cutting strips, a long thin mat can be selected. It is a little less expensive and you will always have a place for it.

I have a small mat that I keep on the ironing board. It is perfect for the second cut right after pressing. The 18" x 24" mat fits perfectly on the kitchen counter when I am working at home and the 24" x 36" mat is on my table in the studio.

Back to the actual cutting process. To be effective in cutting strips with a rotary cutter, you need a strong straight edge. There are many different acrylic rulers 5" or 6" wide and 24" long available. The grid on the ruler surface is very helpful in assuring accuracy. Most rulers also have angles and other special printed features. With just a little practice, you'll be comfortable cutting nearly any straight line geometric shape with just a ruler and rotary cutter. Good-bye templates!

The cutting process can be accomplished with a ruler, pencil and scissors, but with the rotary cutter, protective mat and wide acrylic ruler:

1. You save time measuring. You completely eliminate measuring in from the edge and making dots and then connecting the dots.
2. You save lots of cutting time. The rotary cutter is faster and does more layers at once.
3. You are more accurate. What a bargain!

Even if you don't use a rotary cutter, the minimum new tool should be a wide ruler with increments marked across it allowing you to mark strips easily.

Rotary Cutter Tips

The blades are very sharp. All of the brands currently available have guards. Make sure they are in place when the cutter is not in use. This protects both you and the blade. If you drop the cutter, the blade often becomes nicked. Then instead of cutting the fabric where it is nicked, it perforates. The blades are replaceable, but it is an unnecessary expense if you will just keep the guard in place. A fresh blade will cut 6 to 12 layers of fabric easily with very little pressure. Bearing down too hard is not necessary and can do irreparable damage to the protective mat. It's harder to accurately fold and stack 12 layers of fabric than to cut them.

When cutting, the blade side, not the guard side goes immediately next to the acrylic ruler. Cut away from you, not toward your body.

To get straight lengthwise strips, it is imperative that the ruler be perpendicular to the fold on folded fabrics and parallel to the selvage. The first cut is usually trimming off the selvage (cutting strips on the lengthwise grain) or straightening a store cut edge (cutting strips on the crosswise grain). The next cut is the second side of the first strip. It requires changing hands, going to the other side of the mat, or turning the mat. My favorite method is to cut the first strip left-handed—not really hard with the good ruler—and the rest right-handed which is my favored hand. Then I don't have to change table sides. Take advantage of the grids on the mat and on the ruler to maximize your accuracy.

OTHER TOOLS

Most other tools are probably already in your sewing supplies. Good small scissors, a seam ripper, thimbles, hand-sewing needles, etc. You will probably want to add some specialized quilting tools like removable fabric marking pens and pencils, smaller acrylic rulers and squares soon. Put a steam iron and ironing board next to your sewing machine.

Sewing Techniques

How you actually sew the pieces together unlocks the secrets of "Quilting for People Who Don't Have Time to Quilt" techniques. Eliminate the idea of making a quilt piece by little piece. Remember, everything you can sew before you cut is more accurate, faster and easier!

It's almost revolutionary. It's different from anything you've been taught. This book stresses it repeatedly. You will see how to look at quilt designs you want to make and analyze what pieces you can **sew before you cut.**

CHAIN PIECING STRIPS

The first step in sew-before-you-cut is usually chain piecing strips. When you study a quilt design and see the same two squares of fabric side by side repeatedly, you realize that you can either cut lots of each square and sew them together **or** you can cut a few strips of fabric as wide as the squares, sew the strips together and then cut the sewn strips into pieces as long as the square (**Fig C**).

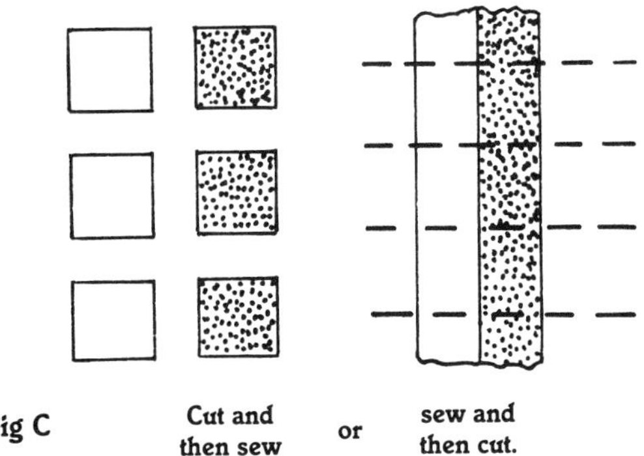

Fig C

When you make Project 1 you will see how to put these simple concepts to work to make you look like a miracle quilter. Your friends will not believe how fast you can do patchwork. You are not required to share these secrets. If, however, you decide to be generous and tell about your newly learned skills, NEVER, NEVER say it's **easy**. Say it's clever, say it's smart, say it's a brilliant new technique you've learned, but never say it's easy. It is, of course, we just don't say so.

CUTTING

We will emphasize thinking ahead. For example, often the first two strips that are going to be sewn together are also the same dimension. If you place the fabrics face to face when you cut, you have eliminated a step and the strips are more accurately positioned for the seam.

THE ACTUAL SEWING

The recommended seam allowance is 1/4", using 10-12 stitches per inch.

It is not necessary to back stitch the seams as you will stitch across most ends almost immediately. If you are new to patchwork, you may not have entered the world of the 1/4" seam allowance yet. After using 5/8" seam allowances in dressmaking, the first 1/4" seam will look impossibly thin. Remember, many 5/8" seam allowances survive being trimmed smaller than 1/4", turned inside out and poked. Not only is the 1/4" seam allowance adequate for patchwork but if it is necessary to make a narrower seam allowance, don't worry until you get below 1/8".

On many sewing machines the outside edge of the presser foot is exactly 1/4" from the center of the needle hole. An easy way to measure is to put a tape measure under your presser foot. Put any inch mark at the needle. Put the presser foot down. If it's 1/4" wide, you're lucky. If it isn't, you'll have to find some way to calculate the 1/4" seam. For now, when you are just doing strips, a guide on the throat plate or a piece of tape can be lined up to show where to run the edge of the fabric. Later, we will be doing things that cover those marks.

SOMETIMES, IT'S CONSISTENCY THAT COUNTS

It is also true that in all the quilts in this book or in any quilt where you are using only strips, even as they become squares, it is consistency that counts. If following the edge of your presser foot makes a seam just a little larger or smaller than 1/4", all that happens is the finished item will be a little larger or smaller, as long as all of the seams are the **same**.

All measurements given in this book are cut measurements. We always talk about the cut size and cut accurately. Then by sewing consistently, the finished sizes are accurate shapes. This is not true with complicated, multi-shaped pieces and curvy lines. With those shapes, you must know exactly what size seam allowance is on the pattern and double check while sewing to be sure you are really stitching on the correct line.

THERE'S MORE TO PERFECT PATCHWORK THAN A 1/4" SEAM ALLOWANCE

In the final analysis, it's the size of what you see that is really important, not the size of the seam allowance. The seam allowance is there to keep the sewing threads from ripping out and to allow you to make adjustments if necessary. The object is to have a perfect 1" square, for example, in the finished patchwork, not to have a perfect 1/4" seam allowance.

MATH VS. PATCHWORK

Math is an exact science—sewing is not. Patchwork is a cross between them. Paper patterns and measurements that are mathematically correct may not end up exact when interpreted in fabrics. It is crucial to learn to find the clues for when it might not be working.

PRESSING—THIS IS NOT AN OPTION!

We sometimes need to be reminded that while members of the current generation are slightly familiar with an iron, they don't know an ironing board's purpose. I bought one for our daughter when she got her first college apartment. The first year she never got it out of the box. The next year it graduated to being an overflow shelf for sweaters.

Make your iron one of your best friends, it is a smart thing to do as you embark on patchwork. My preference is a steam iron.

When pressing seams in patchwork, both seam allowances go in the same direction, not open as in dressmaking. When in doubt, press toward the darker fabric. Time spent carefully pressing is time well spent.

When I am pressing a set of strips, I usually put the strips across the ironing board instead of end to end. With the seam allowances up, I hold onto the fabric with my left hand and put the iron down on the other edge of the strips (**Fig D**). With the weight of the iron holding the fabric, I put just a little tension on the left side, the seam allowances stand up and with the steam iron, I can press them down flat. Keep the strips straight, don't press curves into your strips. I admit to being a fanatic about perfect pressing.

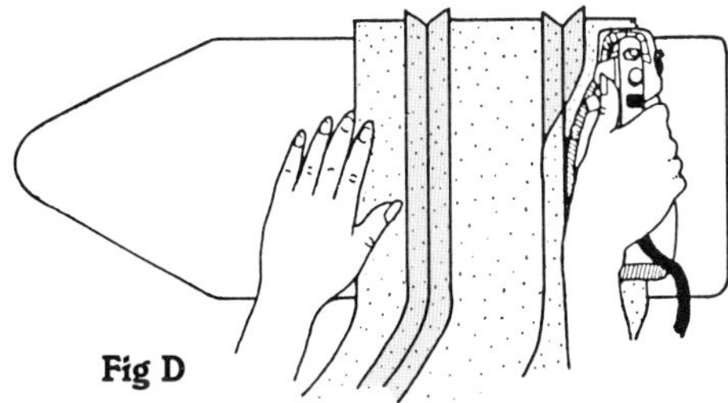

Fig D

With the philosophy that once is not enough, I then turn the strips over and press the printed or right side of the fabric. Again, the seam allowances are going left and when I press against those, I can eliminate any tiny folds I might have pressed into the seam. Tiny 1/32" folds don't seem like much until you multiply that times 2 for each seam and times 4 or 5 seams for a block and times 10 or 12 for the number of blocks.

During the Self-Teaching Projects section, you will see how pressing directionally becomes a crucial part of ease and accuracy in sewing. You will learn how to plan pressing to your advantage. This may not seem very flashy, but it simplifies your stitching life and gives you lots more time for the fun stuff.

Typically, you will press between each step. I don't mind getting up to press. I usually have sewn so many strips or sets together while at the machine that it gives me a chance to stretch.

SHORTCUT PRESSING

Sometimes finger pressing can postpone pressing for one step—but be careful. Sometimes the presser foot tension and your fingers can press the most recent seam adequately. Which is more important to you, perfect, flat seams or saving minutes on every quilt you make the rest of your life?

Everything is a trade off.

THE "SECOND CUT"

This will be your first opportunity to put the **sew-before-you-cut** theories to work. Now that your first strips are cut, pieced and pressed you make the cut that forms the second dimension of the patchwork piece. The width of the strips formed the first dimension. This will be clearer as you make Project 1.

CHAIN PIECING AGAIN

Chain piecing means continuously feeding the same pieces in the same order under the presser foot without cutting the thread. Watch carefully for any obvious visual differences. There are many visual clues. Seams and cut edges should line up perfectly, for example.

TO RIP OR NOT TO RIP

My stitch length is relatively small, and I truly don't like to rip, so my own guideline is rather harsh. If the mistake, once seen, is the first thing I see when I look at the quilt top, I rip. It's not worth being aggravated forever for a few minutes of ripping. If I were planning on entering the quilt in a competition, I'd rip, but competitions aren't really my thing. If I were giving the finished piece away and I thought it wouldn't be noticed, I might not rip. After all, if they found the mistake, they would probably be proud of finding something I had missed—or they would think it was my "humility block". (In some societies, it is believed that as only God could make something perfect, a quiltmaker must make an obvious mistake; hence, humility blocks.)

Some tips on ripping

Sometimes straightening a seam is necessary because there is an equal error in both pieces of fabric. Then straightening simply requires a new seam, no ripping. The old stitching can stay in the seam allowance.

If you must rip, the gentlest way is best. On one side of the seam, cut every 6th stitch or so—a little experimentation will let you know if you can get by with cutting every 7 or 8 stitches. Then turn the fabric over and pull the thread on the other side. When you cut at the right frequency, the thread just pops out as you pull. Go back to the first side and brush away the clipped threads. I can do about 10" per minute or 1/100th of a mile per hour!

In another ripping technique, you pull one thread, gathering the fabric on the seam, until it breaks. Then go to the other side of the fabric and pull the opposite thread until it breaks. Proceed back and forth until the seam is removed. This is faster and neater, but it is harder on the fabric and more likely to cause distortion.

Self-Teaching Projects

The step-by-step projects are presented in a natural progression starting with Project 1, the Five-Strip Fence Rail, and building. Detailed instructions for techniques used in the first project are not repeated in subsequent projects. The most effective way to master these techniques is to make something from every project. If you don't, **please read everything** to develop an understanding of the techniques. Remember the Chinese Proverb:

I hear and I forget.
I see and I remember.
I do and I understand.

Project 1 is especially important (and long) because it covers in detail so many procedures you will use on nearly every quilt in the future. It may seem lengthy because I believe in **complete** instructions. I emphasize good work habits and good basic how-to techniques. You shouldn't have to figure out on your own, procedures I know. It doesn't sound very flashy, but the greatest colors and designs in the world are spoiled by lumpy, bumpy, crooked quilts.

The "Quilting for People Who Don't Have Time to Quilt" techniques are designed to make sure that the quality of your work, justifies your investment of money and time.

Five-Strip Fence Rail

The first project is a full-size quilt. This quilt can be made any size. In fact, the Five-Strip Fence Rail is shown in two sizes and two different arrangements, but PLEASE make a full-size quilt for your first project. You immediately become a quilt maker, you feel great and it impresses your friends immeasurably! Specific instructions are for the multi-colored 80″ x 100″ Five-Strip Fence Rail shown on the front cover. (Variations for the Basket Weave and the Crib Size Basket Weave, photographed on pages 13 and 22, are given at the end.) This may or may not be the perfect quilt for your bedroom. If it is, great. If not, so what? It will make a handsome and impressive wedding or housewarming gift and it is very important to your basic understanding of these techniques.

FABRIC REQUIREMENTS (45″-wide fabrics)

Twenty 3/4-yd pieces of fabric.
Note: If you are buying everything, you need 20 different fabrics for variety and we'll show you a way to use the extra for a simple pieced back. If you are using scraps, see paragraph 1 of "Cutting and Sewing".

3/4 yd for the first border
1 yd for the second border
1 7/8 yd for the third border and binding
bonded polyester quilt batting at least 80″ x 100″
large-eyed, pointed needle and a smooth sport weight yarn—if tying

Some people like to select border fabric after the center is pieced. This allows the finished look of the quilt interior to be part of the selection process. If, however, you are making a multi-colored quilt, that has to "look" a particular color, you should make the border selection now and fulfill that color need. For example, this quilt's borders make it very pink and green. If ecru, slate blue and navy borders had been used instead, it would have been a very blue quilt with pink and green accents.

In fabric selection, light, medium and dark are often more important than actual colors. For this quilt, four definitely light fabrics (they were all ecru or ecru and pink), and four definitely dark fabrics, one each in burgundy, navy, green and brown were chosen first. The other twelve fabrics were selected to develop a compatible range of mediums in the rose, blue and green color families. Notice the variety in the size and types of designs.

ANALYZE—FIND THE UNIT BLOCK

The first thing to find when you are planning how to make a quilt, is the unit block. **The unit block is the smallest repetitive unit.** It doesn't always work but start by looking in the upper left corner. Look to the right until you see the same shape repeating. Then look down from the corner and find the repeat. In these quilts, the unit block (**Fig A**) is a square made with five strips. Only the arrangement of light, medium and dark and the direction of the strips varies. In the Fence Rail, it is light to dark going right to left or top to bottom. In the Basket Weave, the darkest strip is in the middle, flanked by medium and light fabrics. In both quilts, half of the squares are positioned with the strips running vertically and the other half horizontally. There are 130 blocks approximately 6 1/4″ square. Most people would think you cut 650 1 3/4″ x 6 3/4″ strips and start sewing those little pieces together. Cutting strips is right, but we'll use longer strips and will never have to count or handle 650 separate pieces.

Fig A

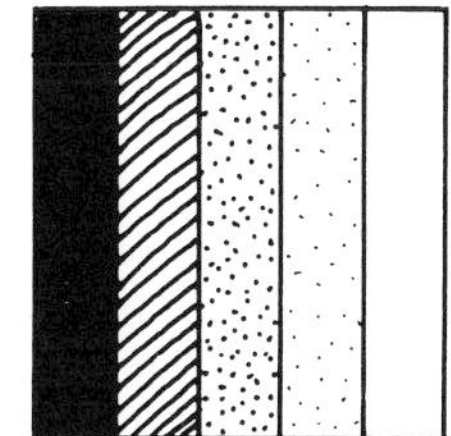

The Unit Block

CUTTING AND SEWING

1. After reading Basic Information on rotary cutting, page 7, cut the 20 selected fabrics according to **Fig B**. There will be 200 strips; 10 strips from each fabric, 1¾" x 27". (If you are using scraps, the minimum, no mistakes number of 1¾" x 27" strips needed is 165.) I like to have extra sets of strips. It gives me reject opportunities and leaves extras for accessories. It's much better to have strips left over than to have to go back and get the fabrics out to cut a few more. Keep light, medium and dark fabrics in three piles.

CUTTING DIAGRAM FOR FIVE-STRIP FENCE RAIL

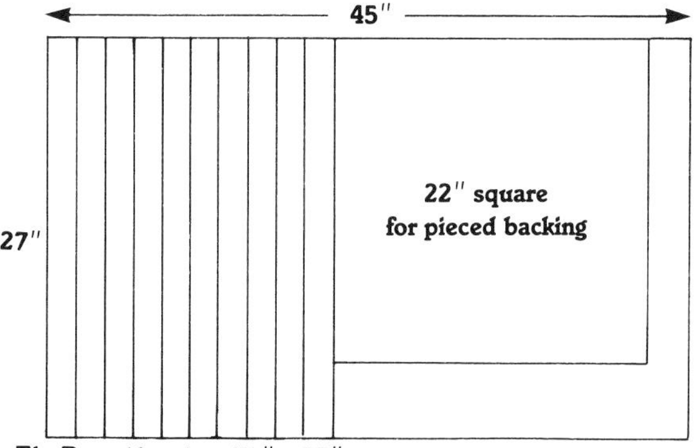

Fig B 10 strips: 1¾" x 27"

2. Remember, **everything you can sew-before-you-cut is easier, more accurate and faster.** Now you will sew five strips together before you cut them to length. You need 40 sets (or 33 using the minimum approach). Start with 40 strips of the darkest fabrics and sew a medium strip to each one. No pinning is necessary. When you finish the first pair, don't stop and cut threads, just feed the next pair right under the presser foot, **Fig C**. It doesn't need to be speed sewing, just a nice steady pace with a consistent seam allowance. You may prefer to press as you go, but it isn't necessary until you have completed sewing all five strips, and it's more efficient to wait.

3. When you have done 40 pairs, start again, adding another medium strip to the second strip, **Fig D**. Make sure the darkest strip is always on the left and the third strip is progressively lighter than the second.

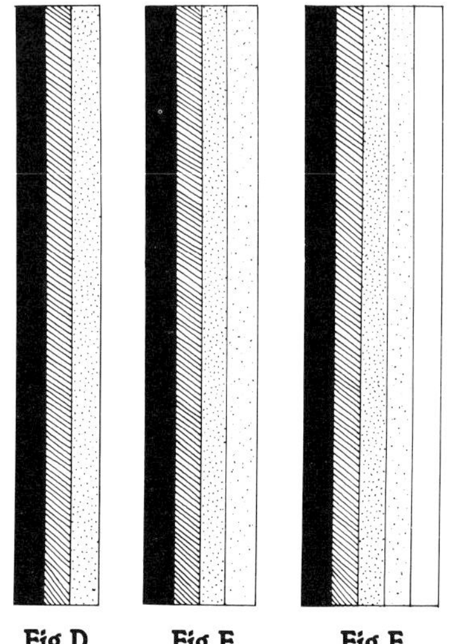

Fig C **Fig D** **Fig E** **Fig F**

The quilt will be more interesting if you vary the arrangements of specific fabrics within the sets of strips while keeping them all dark to light.

4. Add the fourth strip, **Fig E**. It should be lighter than the third, darker than the fifth.

5. Add the fifth strip, **Fig F**, which should be from the fabrics you selected as the lightest.

6. Press all seam allowances in the same direction, toward the darkest strip.

7. Measure across several sets of pressed strips. Theoretically, five 1¾" wide strips sewn with accurate ¼" seam allowances and pressed flat will now be 6¾" wide. If that's what you have, great. If it isn't, the second best thing is to have a consistent finished width, affectionately called your "one and only unique" width. If your strips are all slightly smaller or slightly larger than 6¾", all that happens is your total quilt is slightly smaller or larger. Correct that by adjusting borders or adding another row of strips, if necessary.

If however, the sets are varying widths, it means a lot of adjustments later or a bumpy finished quilt resulting from uneven seams. Double check your pressing. You may have pressed folds in the seams that have made the strip sets uneven and a simple repressing could correct that. Look at the seam allowances. Are they consistent? Check the strips themselves, were they cut evenly? It may be necessary to take out a few seams and adjust. Or if you made extra sets, lay aside the most uneven sets and work with the best.

8. Whether your average width is 6¾" or a one and only unique measurement, it determines the length of your next cut or the **second cut** (as it is sometimes called) and the size of the unit block square. To make these squares, work with one set of sewn strips at a time. With your ruler perpendicular to the long edges and the seams, straighten one end of the strip set. Using the width of the strips as the increment measurement, measure from the newly cut edge, mark and cut or just cut if you are using the rotary cutting system, **Fig G**. You should get four squares from a strip. (In this particular quilt, if you made seam allowances a little too narrow, your set of strips will be greater than 6¾" and you can only get three squares from a set of strips. Cut at least 130 squares. Save any extra pieces. They can be sewn together for pillow ruffles, etc.

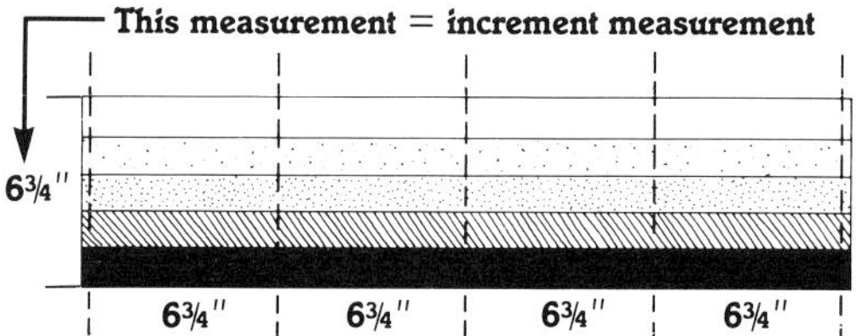

Fig G 6¾" or your one and only unique width

9. It is easiest to do the next step on the floor so you can see the entire arrangement at once. Arrange the blocks as in **Fig H**, 10 blocks wide and 13 blocks long. To develop the fence rail pattern, arrange the horizontal blocks with the dark strip at the bottom and the vertical blocks with the dark strip on the left.

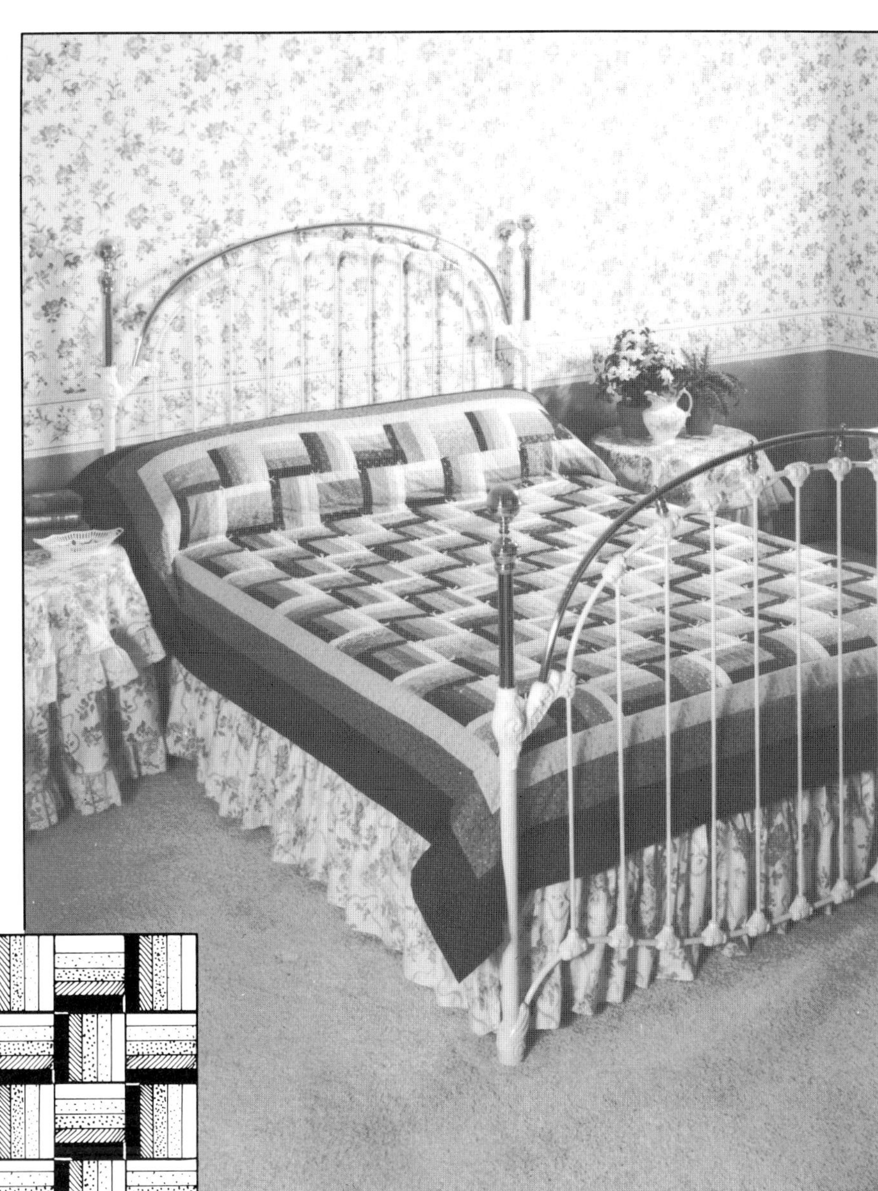

Fig H

Stand back and look. Is there a concentration of color or too many pieces of a particular fabric in one area? Is it well balanced? Are there any mistakes in the order of the blocks? When you are satisfied with the arrangement it's time to start sewing the blocks together. Don't let yourself get crazy with rearranging. The best look on this quilt is a comfortable random look.

10. You are probably thinking that you will sew all ten blocks in the first row together and then the second row and then sew the long rows together, etc. You can, but I prefer a method of sewing pairs of blocks together, then two pairs of blocks, then two pairs of pairs, etc. (**Fig I**). Why? When you sew long strips together you have many seams (in this case, nine) that have to match intersections. If you are off anywhere, it means you have to adjust continually along the seam. When you do pairs, two pairs, etc., you have many seams where there is only one seam intersection to match. It is easy to perfectly match one seam and let any discrepancies fall into the seam allowances.

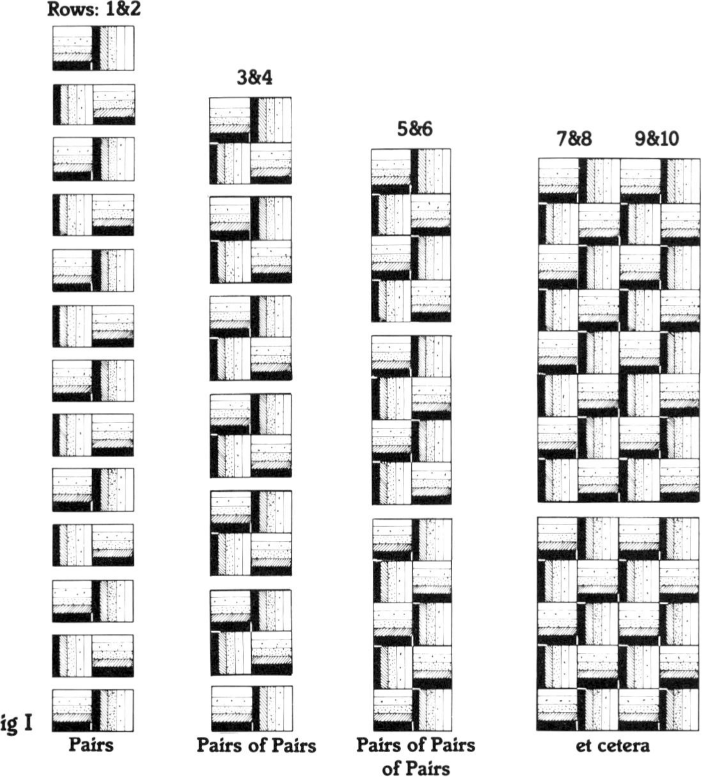

Fig I

To accomplish the pairs method, take each block in the second vertical row and turn it face down on its partner in the first row as if they were already hinged together. That puts them in the proper position for stitching. Then starting at the top of the quilt, pick the pairs up maintaining their correct position and stacking them so that pair #1 is on top of pair #2 which is on top of pair #3, etc.

Hold the blocks in front of you, making sure you don't change hands or position of the blocks! The "hinged" side must stay on the right, the #1 pair on the top! Go to the machine and start stitching the first pair. As you finish that pair, feed the second pair right under the presser foot, and then the third, etc. **Do not cut** the pairs apart, the **chain piecing** will automatically keep them in the correct order. When you have finished vertical rows 1 & 2, repeat with 3 & 4, 5 & 6, etc. It's smart to pin a paper with each row number on the top piece as a reference as you handle the strips, especially if you won't complete this step in one session.

11. As you press the pieced pairs, you can create what I call **automatic pinning.** On each pair, press both seam allowances toward the vertical strips. They will alternate left and right down the row. With your fingers, you can feel the little ridge that develops. Those ridges act like little grippers as you put pairs right sides together for the next seam. With a little practice, as you position the pairs, the ridges just meet, no space between, no overlapping, **no pinning necessary!**

12. Now sew the pairs of pairs. Four unit blocks, but there is still only one seam to match. In a quilt with carefully positioned blocks, it is more important to keep the positioning accurate than to take advantage of chain piecing. Don't cut the thread keeping the vertical rows in line yet, even though it means you need to deal with each seam individually. Because there are 13 horizontal rows, there will be one block left at the end.

13. Now sew pairs of pairs of pairs together. There will be eight unit blocks and still only one intersection to match. Sew the extra pair to the last group of eight on each row.

14. Time to press again. Think ahead. If you press all of the seam allowances in rows 1 & 2 up, 3 & 4 down, 5 & 6 up, etc. you will have automatic pinning as you seam the vertical sections together. All of this leads to a neat flat quilt top. Keep sewing larger units together. The last seam will probably be the horizontal seam between rows 8 & 9. It may seem complicated now, but this planning becomes natural and is worth it in the orderliness that it develops.

15. The interior of the quilt top is now approximately 62½" x 81½". Approximately 10" borders all around will make a great Queen/Double size quilt. The three borders on this quilt are cut 3", 4" and 5" and put on quilt-as-you-sew with blunt (not mitered) corners, **Fig J**. I put my borders on with the quilt-as-you-sew method described on page 44.

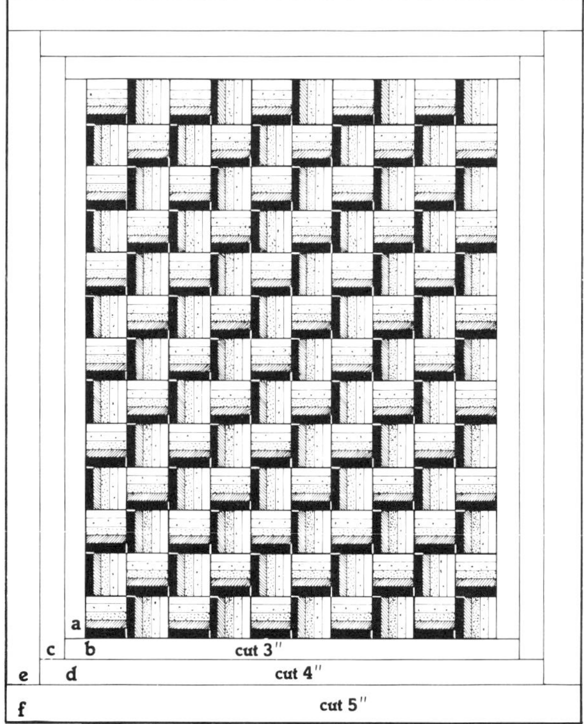

Fig J MATHEMATICALLY CORRECT FINISHED SIZES
Each block : 6¼" sq.
Interior: 62½" x 81¼"
Borders: a. 2½" x 81¼"   d. 3½" x 74½"
b. 2½" x 67½"   e. 4½" x 93¼"
c. 3½" x 86¼"   f. 4½" x 83½"
Quilt with ½" binding: 84½" x 103¼"

Basket Weave Crib Quilt

16. To finish your quilt, read pages 41 to 44. You will need to:

a. Prepare the backing fabric using the 22″ cut squares of quilt top fabrics (allowing 10½″ for borders). Randomly arrange the backing squares four across and five down; refer to photo on page 42. Seam pieces and press seam allowances open.

b. Layer the quilt

c. Tie the interior (or machine quilt it if you prefer)

d. Add the borders in quilt-as-you-sew style

e. Bind the edges

f. Sign the quilt

Now that you understand the time-saving piecing techniques you can apply your new-found knowledge to other variations of the Five-Strip Fence Rail.

VARIATIONS FOR BASKET WEAVE

Instead of the large variety of fabrics, you need only three fabrics for the Basket Weave. We have shown a crib or lap size Basket Weave above. If you would like to make it in a full size, purchase 3 yards of the light and medium fabrics and 1½ yards of the dark fabric. Border fabric requirements are the same as the multi-colored quilt. To cut, I would first cut the fabric into 27″ lengths (the measurement of habit) and then cut the strips on the lengthwise grain.

Think ahead and analyze—In the Basket Weave the light and medium strips are all sewn to each other. For a real savings in time, layer the light and medium fabrics right sides together when cutting the strips—the fabrics are already automatically positioned with the raw edges together for all of the first seams. You can skip the floor method of putting the squares together because all of the blocks are the same. Make 60 pairs with the horizontal strip on the bottom and the vertical on top. Press all the seams toward the vertical block. For the pairs of pairs, turn one pair around and taking advantage of the automatic pinning, seam the units of four into the correct position. At this point, you may want to put the blocks on the floor to get the proper 10 row by 13 row arrangement. Finishing and borders are the same as the Five-Strip Fence Rail.

These instructions seemed very long, but it won't be long before this limited statement would be all you would need to make this quilt. "Interior of cover quilt is 10 units by 13. The strips are cut 1¾″ and the borders are cut 3″, 4″ and 5″. In fact, you can probably do it now.

VARIATIONS FOR THE BASKET WEAVE CRIB QUILT

The crib or lap quilt, photographed above and on page 22, has 35 units, (5 x 7). The strips are cut 1¾″. It has a single border cut 4½″ wide and a ¾″ finished binding.

Sticks and Stones

This quilt is called Sticks and Stones because it sounds so much more interesting than its old name, Strips and Squares. It is a simple variation of the Fence Rail. It is a three-strip Fence Rail block alternating with an empty square. I suggest that you read through this entire project before you start. I've also given instructions for a diagonal set Sticks and Stones.

FABRIC REQUIREMENTS (45″-wide fabrics)

For the 45″ sq pink and blue Sticks and Stones (shown on pages 17 and 22)

- 1¼ yds Lightest fabric—used in strips, squares and outside border
- ¾ yd Medium fabric—middle border and middle strip of small strips
- 1¼ yds Darker fabric
- ⅜ yd Medium fabric used as first border
- 3 yd fabric for backing

For the diagonal set Sticks and Stones Wall hanging—approx. 36″ sq (shown on pages 20 and 23)

No more than ¾ yd (my basic speculative purchase) of any fabric is needed for this quilt. This is another reason I like the 27″ purchase. It is enough to complete most smaller quilts that use at least four fabrics and many full-size quilts using nine or ten fabrics.

ANALYZE—FIND THE UNIT BLOCK

Look for the unit block. Start in the upper left-hand corner. Remember, it doesn't always work, but it often does. Look to the right until you see the same piece appear. Go back to the corner and look down until the same piece appears. In this quilt, when the same piece appears, it is going the opposite direction, **Fig A**. When you look closely, there is an extra row of blocks at the right and at the bottom of the quilt, **Fig B**. There's a reason. I call it **The Rule of the Matching Corners.** As you study quilts, you will discover that any design that has alternate unit blocks is more appealing if all the corners have the same unit. It completes the design, and keeps it in balance. This quilt is your first example of finding the extra rows. When the units blocks are all alike, as in the Fence Rail or Basket Weave, matching corners are not as important.

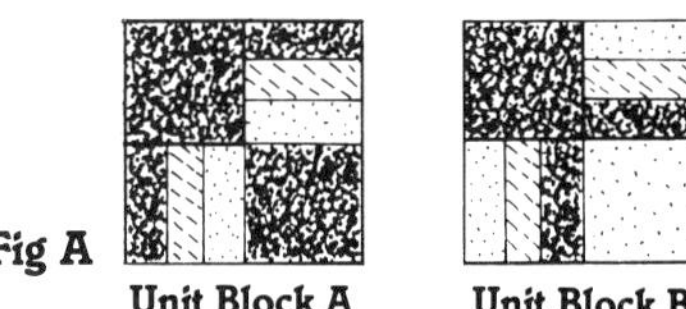

Fig A

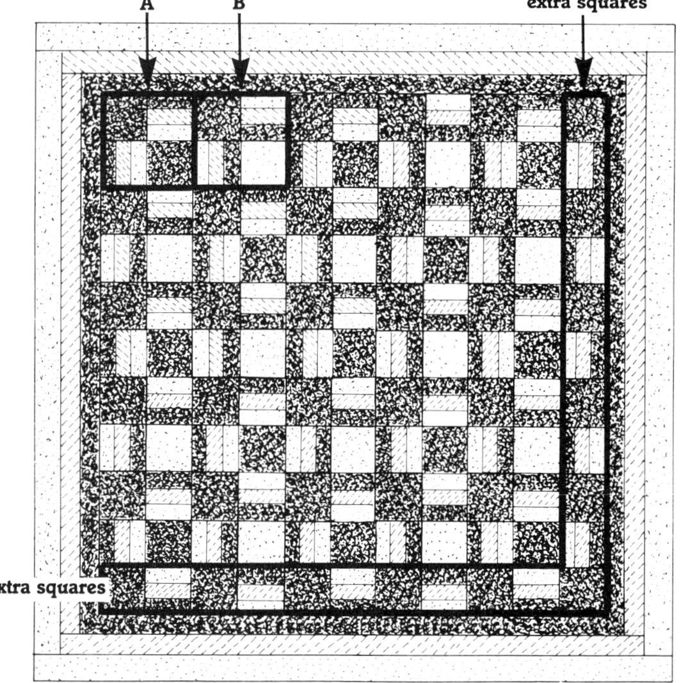

Fig B

After the unit is defined, break it down into smaller parts—always looking to be efficient in construction techniques—to think smarter.

Sticks and Stones Wall Hanging

CUTTING AND SEWING

1. Cut and sew the strips for this quilt. You can get the same design with any width strip, but to make this exact quilt, cut 1½" strips. Cut multiple layers. Remember, fabrics that are to be cut in matching size strips and seamed can be layered with their right sides together for cutting. You save lots of time in the sewing process by never needing to position those two strips for sewing. Think ahead and think smarter.

2. Now you are ready to cut the set of sewn strips into squares. Wait a minute! For the half of each unit block that looks like this [icon] as in 2nd step, c and d below, why not sew the square on in strip form? Anything that you can sew before you cut is quicker, easier and more accurate. Sew the strip that will be an empty square to the three strips. What size will that strip be? **Measure.** Remember, we don't care if three 1½" strips, properly cut, properly sewn and properly pressed will theoretically be 3½" wide. Don't cut the new strip the size it **should** be, make it match the sewn sets. After sewing, press all seams toward the empty square. Take the set to the cutting board and you are cutting four pieces at one time!! When you cut them together, they match! What size will you cut? To make a square, the length of the cut will be the same as the width of the sewn set of three strips which also equals the strip you just cut for the empty square.

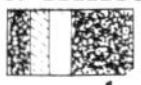

3. With the other half of the unit block, the three pieced strips have to be pressed, cut to make a square, turned and sewn to the wide strip. Then press toward the empty block and cut the strip the same size as the cut section.

4. Now, sew pairs of pairs together. You still have just one seam to match and because you have practiced selective pressing, you have established automatic pinning at every intersection. In other words, the seam allowances go in opposite directions. Proceed to complete the quilt top and finish as desired. The borders on the pink and blue quilt pictured are cut 1¾", 1¾" and 1⅞".

INTRODUCTION TO SPEED PIECING DIAGRAMS

This is how I like to analyze the patchwork in diagrams. It shows in diagram form the breakdown of pieces for Sticks and Stones quilt shown on pages 16 and 17.

1st step—Cut and sew:

a. strips to equal 60

Cut:

b. strips to equal 49

c. strips to equal 12

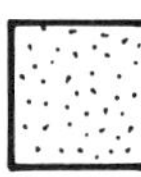

2nd step—Chain piece:

a. 17

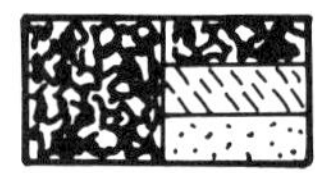

(13 are for Unit Block A, 4 for extra rows)

b. 18

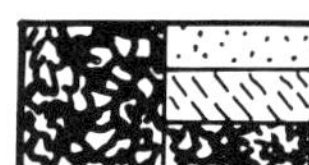

(12 are for Unit Block B, 6 for extra rows)

c. 13

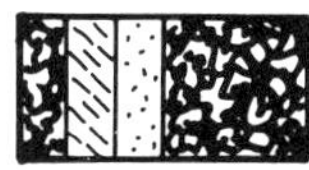

d. 12

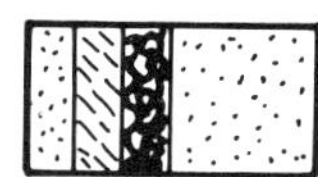

e. 1

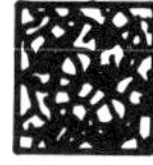

3rd step—
Assemble 13 Unit Block A, 12 Unit Block B and extras. Either follow diagram carefully or put quilt out on the floor to check the design and continue putting subunits and unit blocks together.

Fig C — Diagonal Set Sticks and Stones Wall Hanging

INTRODUCTION TO DIAGONAL SET QUILTS

When the unit blocks are set on point instead of resting flat on a side, that is called a diagonal set. Look at the same unit blocks set on the diagonal, **Fig C**. The rows developed by the blocks go diagonally across the quilt. It's a great look and you need fewer blocks to make the same size quilt because the setting triangles fill so much space. Turn your head or turn the book to see the rows flat.

There are many things to learn about diagonal set quilts, but for this book, we are only going to cover one trick. This is the **Secret of the Setting Triangles.**

I have said that everything in this book is made from strips or squares and the setting triangles are no exception. To cut a square in half diagonally and get two triangles is not a secret. However, it may be disastrous because the hypotenuse or long side of the triangle is now on the bias and we have already determined that that is undesirable. To make the setting triangles, we are going to make a larger square and cut it in **quarters** diagonally, **Fig D**. Now the hypotenuse is on the straight grain. So analyze your right angle triangles. If you want the hypotenuse to be on straight grain, quarter a square diagonally. If you want the legs or short side to be on the straight grain as in the corners of this quilt, halve a square diagonally, **Fig E**.

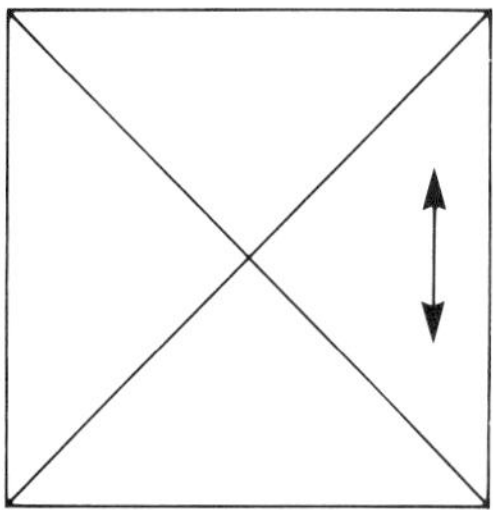

Fig D

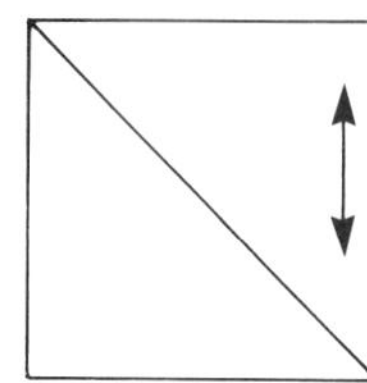

Fig E

What size is the square you plan to quarter? The side of the square should be 7/8" longer than the **diagonal** of the unit block or design block that it touches for an exact, no mistakes fit. I prefer to make the setting blocks larger so that the design blocks float inside the borders instead of being crushed by them. For floating, make the side of the square 1½" to 2½" longer than the diagonal of the unit block.

After all the unit blocks are made and the setting triangles cut, diagonal set quilts are put together in straight rows that run diagonally across the quilt, **Fig F**. Because the center row is a different width, the corners are not the same size as the setting triangles.

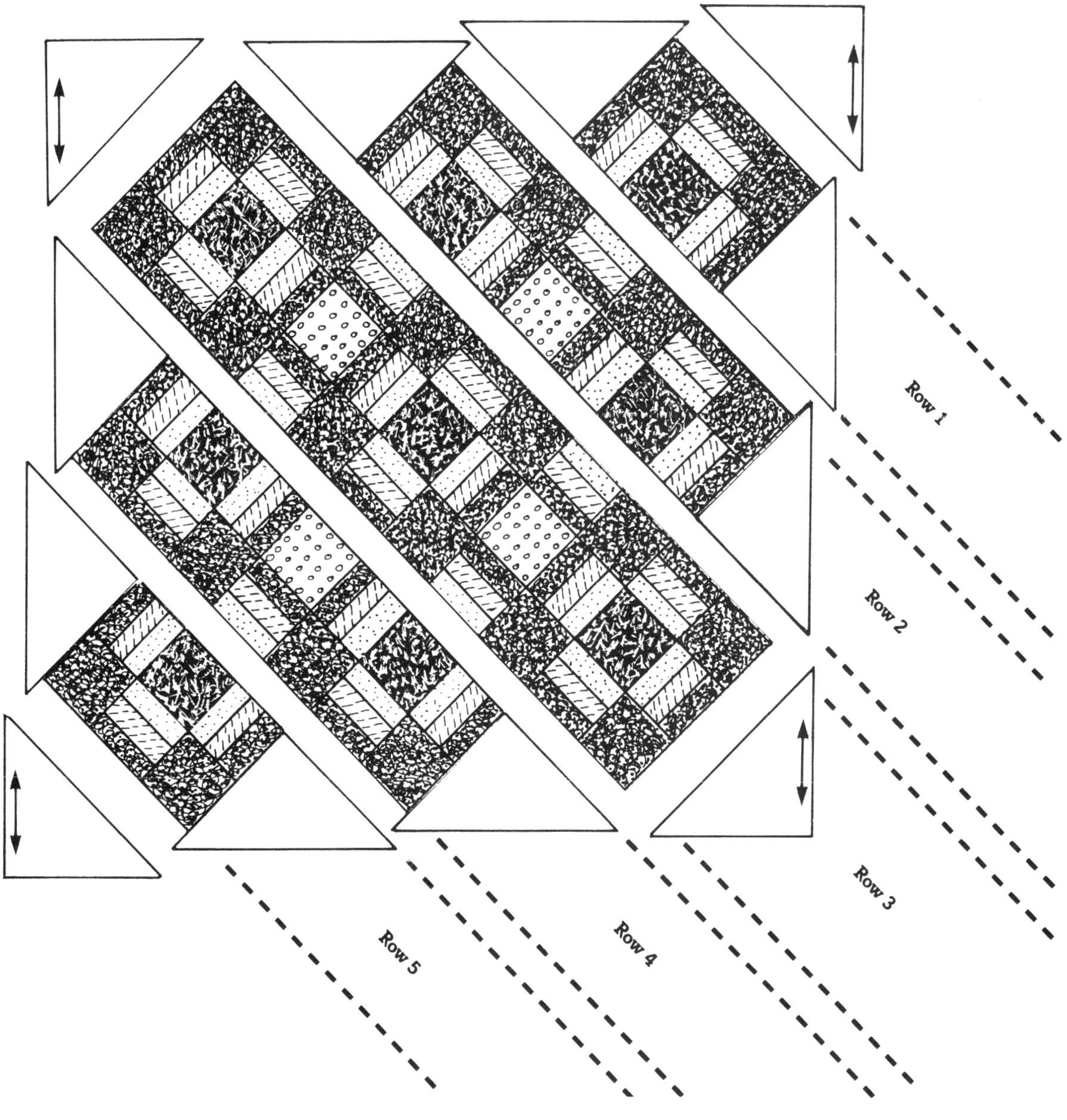

Row 1

Row 2

Row 3

Row 4

Row 5

Fig F

No-Name Four Patch printed panel wall hanging – Project 3, page 25

On the wall: Floral Bouquet Nine Patch – Project 4, page 29
On the bed: Double Irish Chain in Glendale Gardens fabrics – Project 5, page 34

Top left: Crib Size Basket Weave –
Project 1, page 15
Top right: Sticks and Stones –
Project 2, page 16
Lower left: Double Irish Chain –
Project 5, page 34
Lower right: Red, White and Blue
Mini Nine Patch – Project 4, page 29

Amish Magic Nine Patch – Project 4, page 32

Top: Diagonal Set Sticks and Stones –
Project 2, page 16
Lower left: Double Irish Chain –
Project 5, page 34

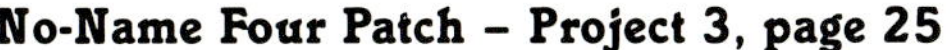

No-Name Four Patch – Project 3, page 25

Magic Nine Patch in hand-dyed fabrics – Project 4, page 32

Crib-size Magic Nine Patch – Project 4, page 32

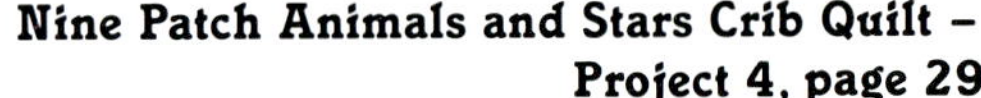

Nine Patch Animals and Stars Crib Quilt – Project 4, page 29

Double Irish Chain Wall Hanging or Tablecloth – Project 5, page 34

PROJECT 3

No-Name Four Patch

This project includes discussion of three photographed quilts: No-Name Four Patch in red/ecru fabrics, No-Name Four Patch in peach/seafoam fabrics and a wall hanging using printed panel fabrics.

FABRIC NOTES—for the 32" square without borders (two quilts shown in red/ecru and peach/seafoam on page 23).

For the interior piece on both the red/ecru and peach/seafoam quilts, you can barely squeak by with no mistakes with 5/8 yd of fabric for the two interior fabrics. Since I usually have a minimum of 3/4 yd there is plenty, except for the border.

You need a minimum of 1 1/8 yd of fabric if it is used in the interior **and** the border with borders cut crosswise, so I would go ahead and buy 1 1/4 yd of fabric and cut my borders lengthwise with no piecing needed.

FABRIC NOTES—for printed panel wall hanging

This wall hanging, shown on page 21, has seven different fabrics. The yardage for the printed panels would be determined by their size and positioning. Once they are selected, the length of one printed block is the amount of fabric needed for the three interior fabrics.

Your choice of borders (how many, how wide, etc.) will determine the yardage. By now, you certainly know I would prefer lengthwise grain. However, when a border is 3" wide and less than 45" long and the fabric is not being used in the quilt, I can either buy 3/8 yd and cut crosswide borders, or I can insist on lengthwise and buy 1 1/4 yds.

ANALYZE—FIND THE UNIT BLOCK

The No-Name Four Patch combines two sizes of squares and strips. There are two unit blocks. They are identical except the fabrics are reversed. Both have a big square, two vertical rectangles (strips), two horizontal rectangles (strips) and four little squares commonly called a four patch, **Fig A**. With what you know and only two measurements, 2" and 4 1/2", you could make a duplicate quilt. Perhaps you are thinking you don't want a red and ecru quilt. Then look at the peach quilt. It's exactly the same, but looking at these two quilts together dramatically demonstrates the importance of fabric selection to the mood of the quilt. Even though both quilts have the very same size and shape pieces, the red and ecru quilt is strong, graphic, high contrast, country, masculine. While the low contrast, soft colors, and the large print in the peach and seafoam quilt gives it a soft, romantic, wicker garden room look.

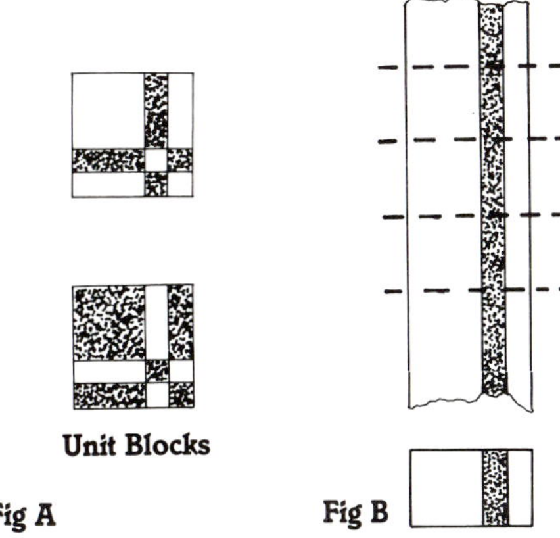

Fig A Fig B

The shapes don't have to be the same proportion. In the brown and gold quilt, instead of 2" and 4 1/2", the proportions are 1 1/4" and 8". Still the very same shapes, squares and rectangles, but different proportions, and instead of just two colors, this version has four. Are you getting the picture? Once you learn the methods, you can vary the sizes and proportions, fabrics and number of colors and make the same quilt 10 times before anyone else in the family will catch on!

P.S. Isn't this a fun way to use the printed panels? It was, of course, the size of the printed picture that determined the 8" measurement and personal choice the 1 1/4" strip. Remember, with these techniques, measurements are always cut sizes, not finished sizes.

CUTTING AND SEWING

1. Cut and sew the thin strips and press to the dark. Did you remember to put the two fabrics right sides together when cutting? It's very important to keep reinforcing the techniques with each quilt. It's obvious that the rectangles are made from strips, but so is the large square. Make strips as long as the cut square measurement and sew one to the pair of narrow strips (**Fig B**), on the correct side, of course. Cut all three at once, **Fig B**. It is much easier to be accurate with a cut this wide using the rotary cutter system. With one cut, the top section of the unit is done.

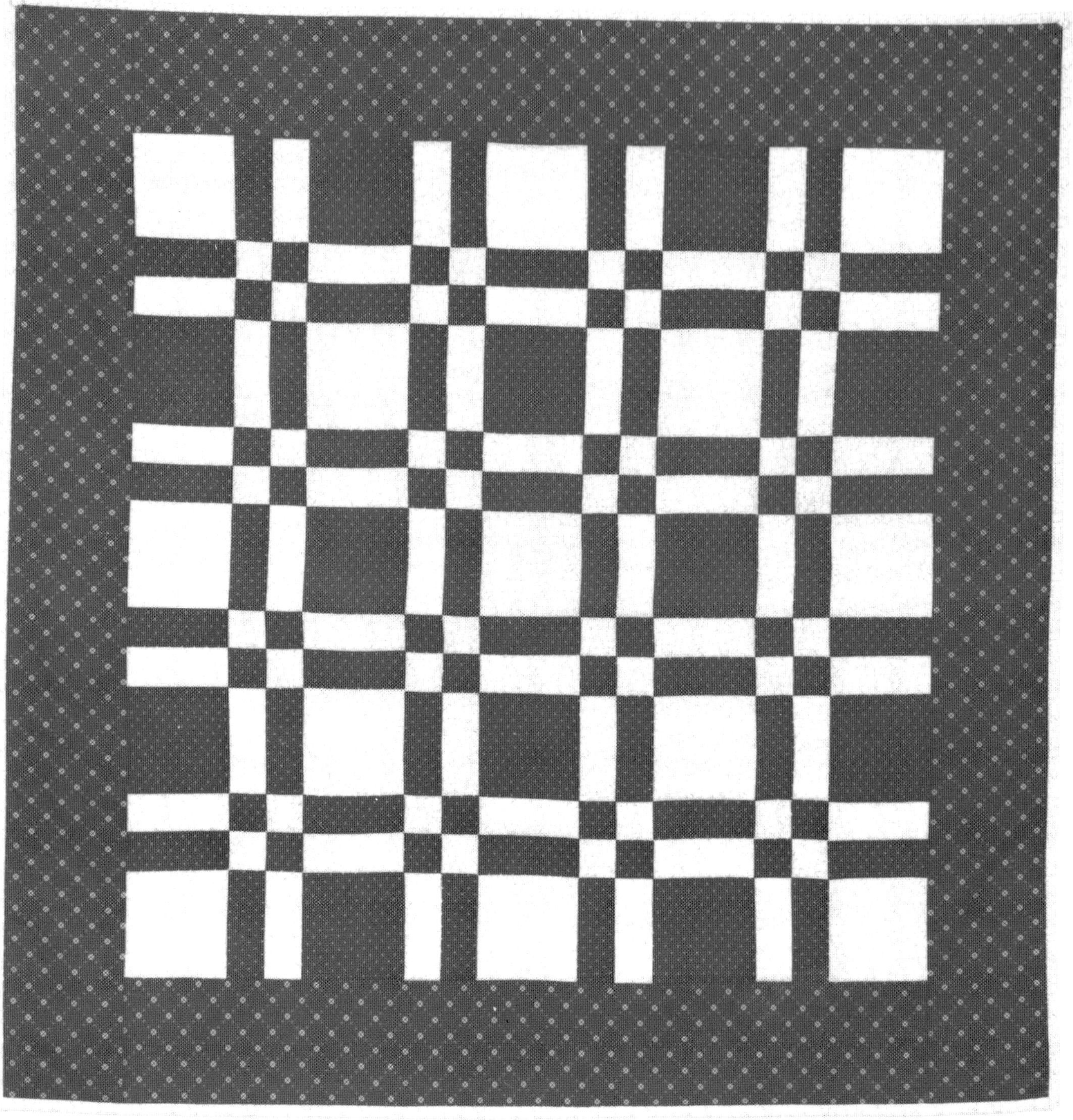

No-Name Four Patch in red/ecru fabrics

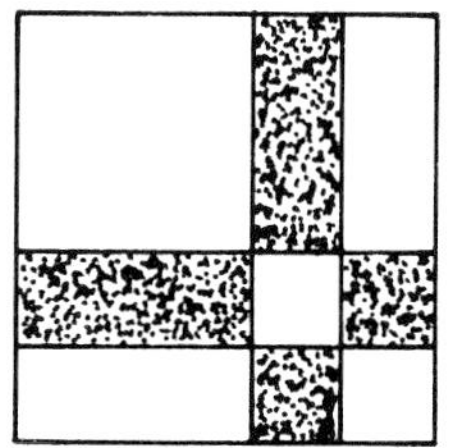

Unit Block

2. Cut more of the sewn narrow strips into rectangles for the bottom section (**Fig C**) and all that is left to make is the four patch!! This is where you can become an instant star! Anyone can see the four patch is tricky. If you make crisp neat four patches or checkerboards, you must be good!

It is obvious that the pieces in the four patch are the same size as the narrow strips. So, using the narrow strips, sew two contrasting fabrics together and press to the dark. Repeat. Position the two pairs of strips right sides together, with opposite fabrics touching, **Fig D**. Two 27" strips can be properly positioned almost as fast as two small pieces. Using the width of the individual strips as the increment, cut through both sets of strips, **Fig E**. They are cut in pairs, properly positioned and ready to sew. For this quilt, you need 16 four patches. So cut 16 pairs of pairs, take the whole stack to the machine and chain piece, **Fig F**. Take advantage of the automatic pinning developed from seam allowances pressed in opposite directions. Isn't that slick? And it comes with **The Four Patch Guarantee:** "You can spend more time making four patches and you can do it more difficultly, but you can't be any more accurate."

Layering pieced sets of strips right sides together and cutting so they are prepositioned for chain piecing is particularly suited to the rotary cutter because the fabrics stay flat during the cutting process.

3. Chain piece four patches and horizontal strips to complete the lower section of the block, **Fig G**. Check, double check and go for it with chain stitching. If you're wrong, you're consistently wrong—and you can either develop a new design or chain rip!

4. Then chain piece the two sections together until you have eight of each unit block, plus the extra pieces for the extra row on one side and the bottom. After chain piecing, I like to leave the units connected while pressing and cut them apart later on a grid marked mat with the rotary cutter and acrylic ruler. That gives me a chance to make minor adjustments if needed.

5. Border as you like. The small quilts are all bordered differently to fit the mood and design as advantageously as possible. The borders shown for all the quilts are just starting points. Eliminate a color or add another fabric if you like the quilt better. Borders are like mats and a frame on pictures. There is no single size that would be perfect regardless of color, nor single color that would be perfect in spite of size variance.

Most often I add borders quilt-as-you-sew, as described on page 44. However, if you want to put borders on traditionally, now is the time. This is one of the few places it is necessary to measure. Measure all sides of the quilt top. Is it symmetrical? If so, cut the borders to fit, pin them in place and make the edges match. Some people cut longer borders and just sew until they run out of quilt edge. Too often this allows stretching and the edges are no longer symmetrical.

If the edges did not quite match, you can perfect the size now. Make matching borders the length of the shorter side. Ease the longer side into the short border. Add both sides, then the ends. Always add multiple borders in the same sequence.

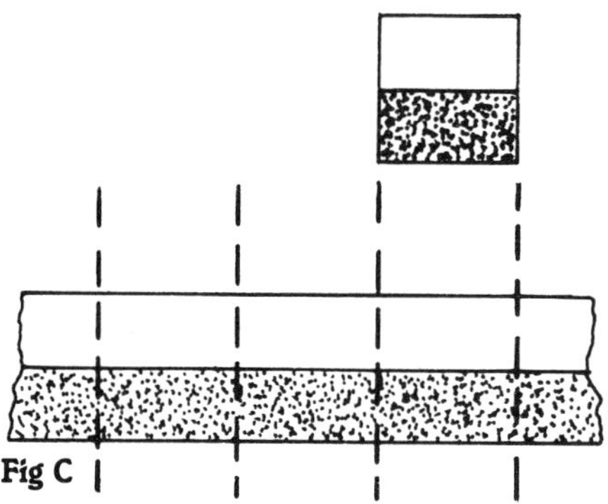
Fig C

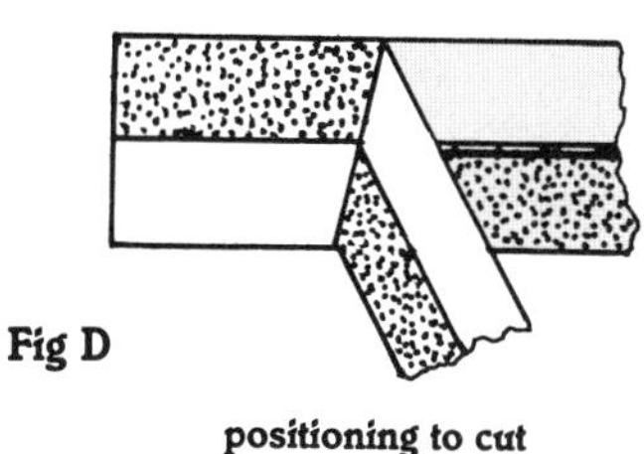
Fig D

positioning to cut

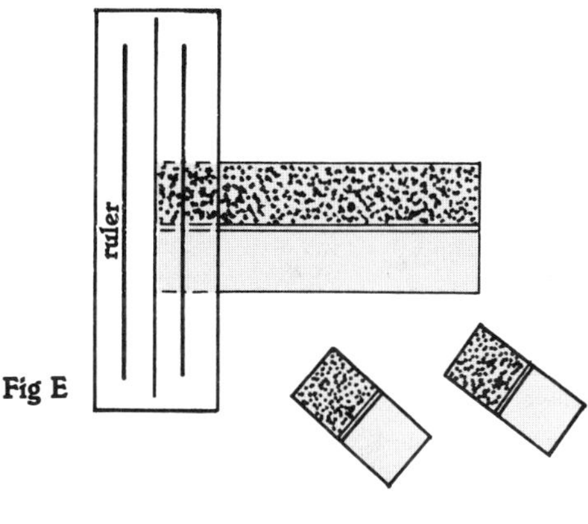

Fig E

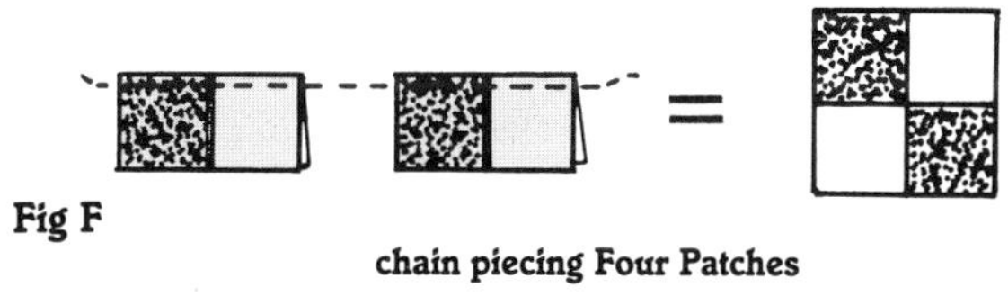
Fig F

chain piecing Four Patches

Fig G

No-Name Four Patch in peach/seafoam fabrics

No-Name Four Patch using printed panel fabrics

SPEED PIECING DIAGRAMS

For red/ecru or peach/seafoam wallhangings:

Step 1: Cut and sew 2 narrow strips and 1 larger strip to equal

8 and 8

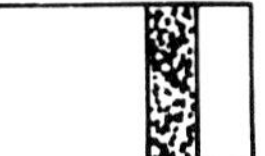

in addition,

24 5

16 4

Step 2:

8

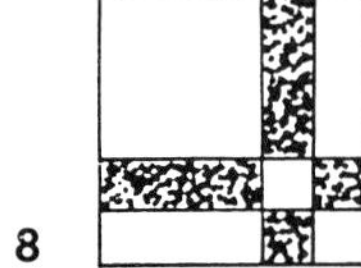

8

4

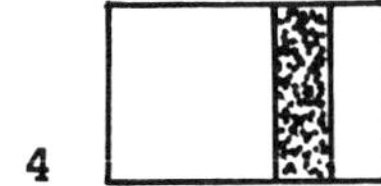

4

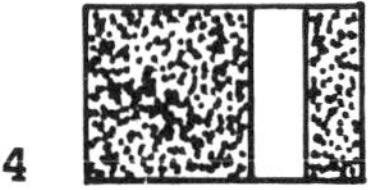

1

Nine Patch Bonanza

This project includes discussion of seven photographed quilts: Floral Bouquet Nine Patch, Heart Panel Nine Patch, Animal and Stars Crib Quilt, Red/White/Blue Mini diagonal set Nine Patch, Magic Nine Patch in Hand-dyed fabrics, Amish Magic Nine-Patch and Crib-size Magic Nine Patch.

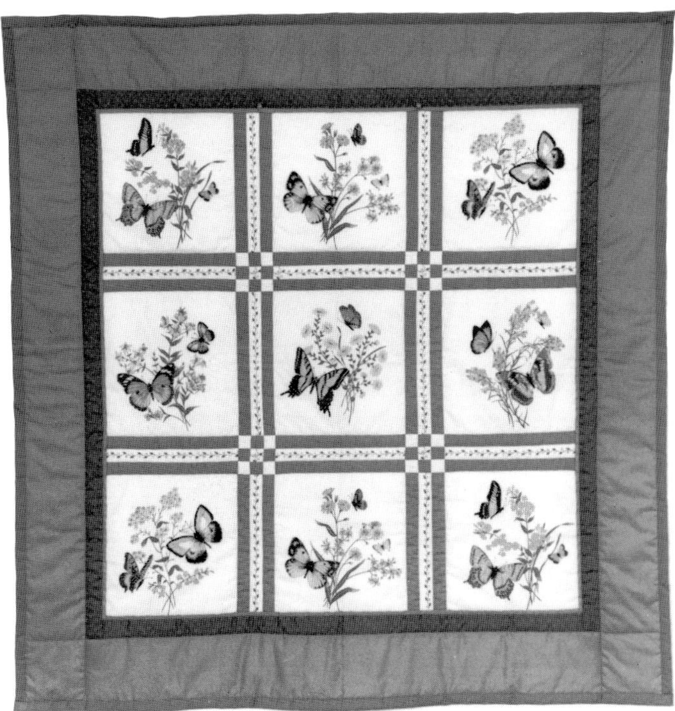

Floral Bouquet Nine Patch

FABRIC NOTES – for Floral Bouquet Nine Patch (here and on page 21) and Heart Panel Nine Patch (here and on back cover)

Printed panels are so popular. A great trick for making quilts from them is to set them with three strip sashing that makes nine patches at every intersection. Both the Heart Panel and the Floral Bouquet are great examples. So easy, yet so great looking. Strip widths are selected to be pleasing with the printed design. The cut strip width determines the size of the pieces for the second cut. The size of the printed panel determines the length of the strip.

Heart Panel Nine Patch

Animal and Stars Nine Patch

Red, White and Blue Mini Quilt

FABRIC NOTES—for Animals and Stars Crib Quilt
(shown on pages 24 and 30)

This fun child's quilt was made to show a version of nine patch intersections and three-strip sashing. It's a reminder that fabric doesn't have to be little itsy-bitsy to go in a quilt. It's okay to cut trees in half. This quilt took 5/8 yd of white and 1/2 yd of blue for the top. It is tied with variegated yarn to accent the fabric colors. Made with a 10¼" square and 1⅞" strip, cut sizes.

FABRIC NOTES—for Red, White and Blue Mini-Quilt
(shown on pages 22 and 30)

The diagonal set red, white and blue mini-quilt has twelve little nine-patches, with 1½" cut strips. The smaller the pieces you are working with, the happier you should be about these techniques. I guarantee that the strip techniques give you more accurate nine patches than cutting and piecing one square at a time. The great imbedded effect is achieved by using the same fabric in the alternate square and the "background" of the nine patch. The quilt is set diagonally (see page 19), it floats, is machine quilted in the center and hand quilted in the border. Its 17½" x 20½" size was designed to resemble an antique doll quilt. You might look at this little quilt and wonder why I didn't hand quilt it all—it couldn't take more than a couple of hours. But in two hours I could make two more little quilts, trying out other colors or fabrics. Besides, the prints are so busy that even with the hand quilted border, you don't really miss the hand quilting in the center. The border is a perfect example of what can happen when you decide a simple hand quilted chain would look good. Before you know it, a single chain has turned into a double chain and instead of quilting around the quilt twice, it's four times. That is both a joy and aggravation of hand quilting. It is easy to imagine how just one more row of quilting would look so good!

ANALYZE, CUT AND SEW

Now that you can make four patches, you know how to make nine patches, too. Just one more row of strips in each direction. Nine patches can be made into great quilts or are zippy accents. As you look through quilt books, you'll start seeing the nine patch repeat everywhere.

To make the nine patch, make a set of strips for each row, **Fig A**. Rows 1 and 3 are the same. Press to the dark and place pressed rows 1 and 2 right sides together just like the four patch, **Fig B**. Cut and chain piece, **Fig C**. Cut threads and add row 3, **Fig D**.

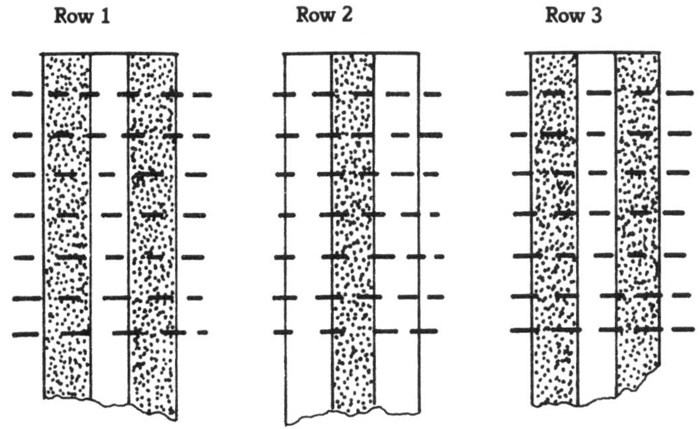

Fig A

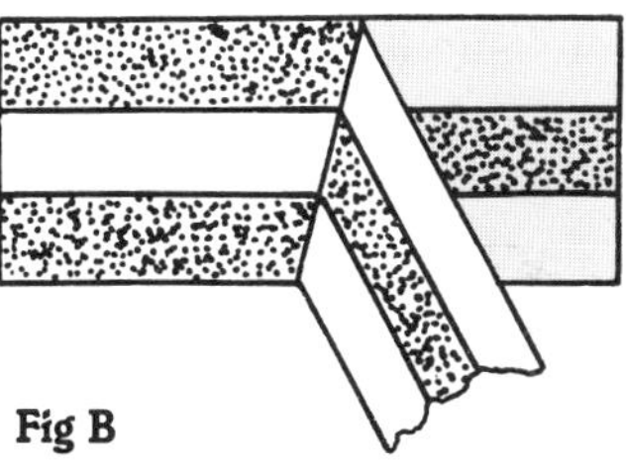

Fig B

Fig C

Fig D

Fig E

Magic Nine Patch

FABRIC REQUIREMENTS — for wall hanging of hand-dyed fabrics (shown on pages 23 and 33)

This quilt has a 3″ cut strip with a finished quilt size of approximately 46″ square.

⅞ yd minimum for background fabric
(I would buy 1⅜ yd and cut borders on lengthwise grain)
½ yd of dark blue fabric
⅜ yd of lt blue fabric
¼ yd of rose fabric (strips for first border are cut crosswise)

ANALYZE — FIND THE UNIT BLOCK

In the Magic Nine Patch, alternate nine patch blocks are colored differently and set diagonally to develop an all over pattern that completely defies its simplicity, **Fig E**. There is a common fabric in both blocks that develops the background for the chain effect. All three models, the small Amish wall hanging, the yellow, green and pink crib quilt and the larger wall hanging made with hand-dyed fabrics, have pieced setting triangles to continue the pattern all the way to the borders. For a variety in looks, the borders were added differently.

When looking for unit blocks in a diagonal set quilt, it is helpful to tilt either the quilt or your head so that the blocks are sitting on their side. All of the quilts have two unit blocks.

CUTTING AND SEWING

Width of the first cut strips from smallest quilt to largest: Amish 1½″, Crib 3″ and Hand-dyed 3″. Borders vary to best suit the quilt.

Plan your pressing to develop automatic pinning. When making the nine patches, press toward the common background fabric whether it is the darkest or not. When joining the nine patches, press toward the setting triangles and the alternate nine patch (the one that has the least unit blocks).

SPEED PIECING DIAGRAM

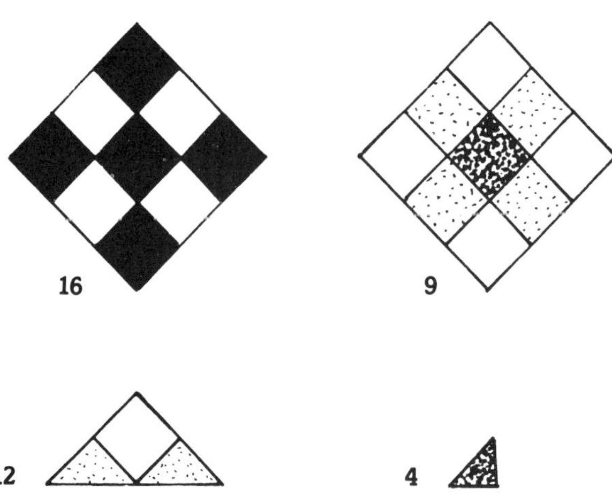

The small triangles in the setting triangles should be cut like the setting triangles for the diagonal set quilt, page 19.

To make the shirred border on the crib quilt, cut the border twice as long as outside dimension of quilt and 4″ to 5″ wide. Gather evenly on both sides. Make sure gathers are perpendicular to quilt and don't angle.

Add the narrow straight borders to the gathered edges and then handle as a unit. Corners were overlapped and excess fabric trimmed away; then corners were stitched in place by hand.

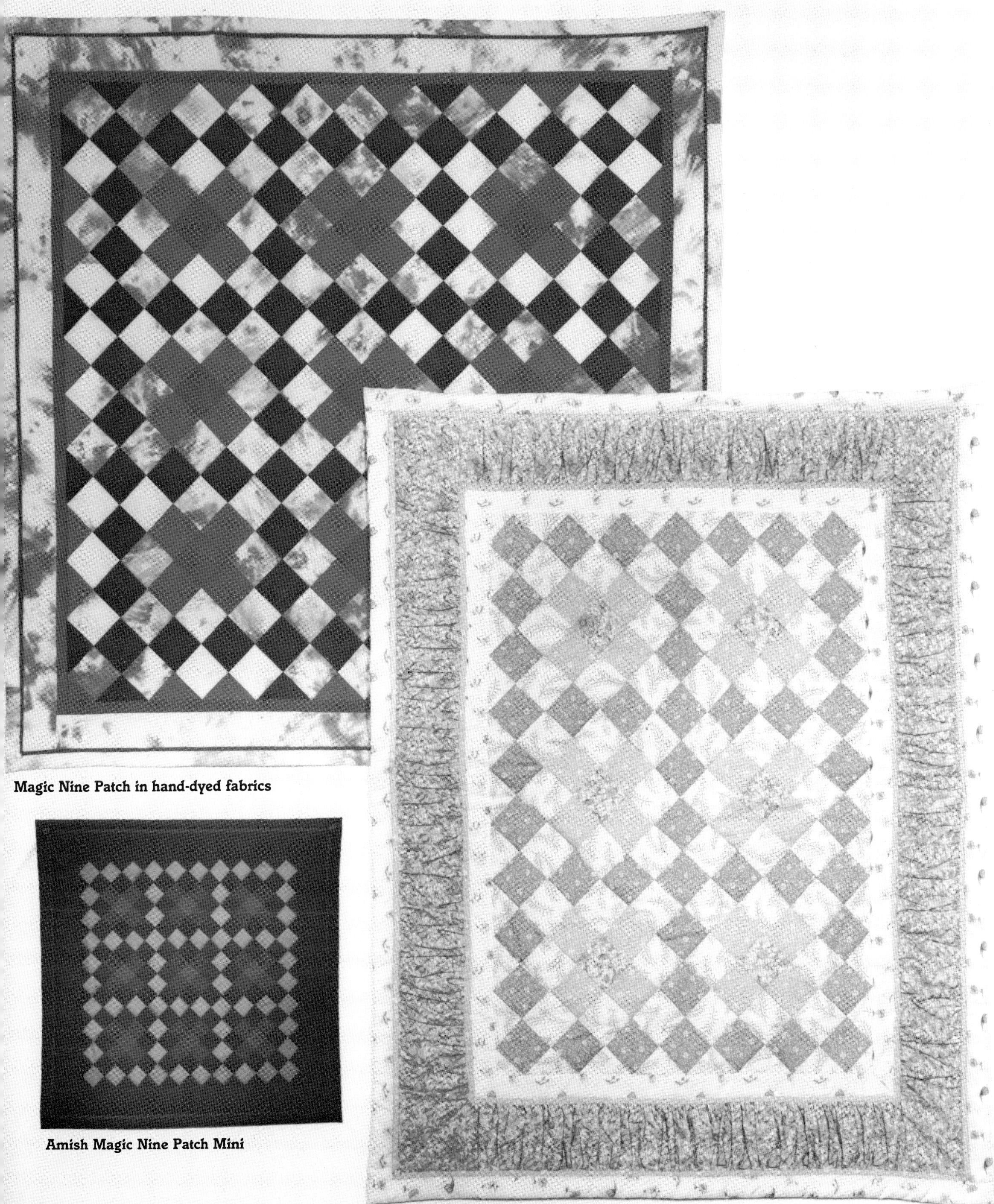

Magic Nine Patch in hand-dyed fabrics

Amish Magic Nine Patch Mini

Crib-size Magic Nine Patch

Double Irish Chain

This project includes discussion of five photographed quilts: Rose and Muslin Double Irish Chain, Glendale Gardens Double Irish Chain, and three Double Irish Chain Wall Hangings or Tablecloths.

FABRIC REQUIREMENTS (45″-wide fabrics)

For Rose and Muslin Queen/Double Size Quilt (shown on page 35 and back cover)

- 1¼ yds Dark fabric
- 2¼ yds Medium fabric
- 3½ yds Light fabric
- Strips: 2½″ cut, 2″ finished
- For borders: ½ yd of Muslin (cut crosswise for first border, cut 1⅜″ wide), ⅝ yd Light fabric (for second border, cut 2¾″ wide, 1 yd of Medium fabric (for third border, cut 4″ wide).

FABRIC REQUIREMENTS (45″-wide fabrics)

For Glendale Gardens Queen/Double Size Quilt (shown on pages 21 and 35)

- 1 yd Dark fabric
- 1¾ yds Medium fabric
- 2 yds Light fabric
- Strips: 3″ cut, 2½″ finished
- For borders: These borders were cut special to take advantage of printed designs and were cut on the lengthwise grain. The first border was cut 2⅝″ wide; the second border was cut 7½″.

Note: The pillow cases and pillow shams shown in the photo on page 21 were made from the same fabrics as the quilt, and require extra fabric.

FABRIC REQUIREMENTS (45″-wide fabrics)

For the three Double Irish Chain wall hangings or square tablecloths (shown on pages 22, 23, 24 and 37)

Buy 1 yd, ⅝ yd, and ⅜ yd of appropriate fabrics for interior blocks, plus at least ½ yd for borders. A 2″ cut strip, five blocks wide and five blocks high with appropriate borders makes a nice wall hanging.

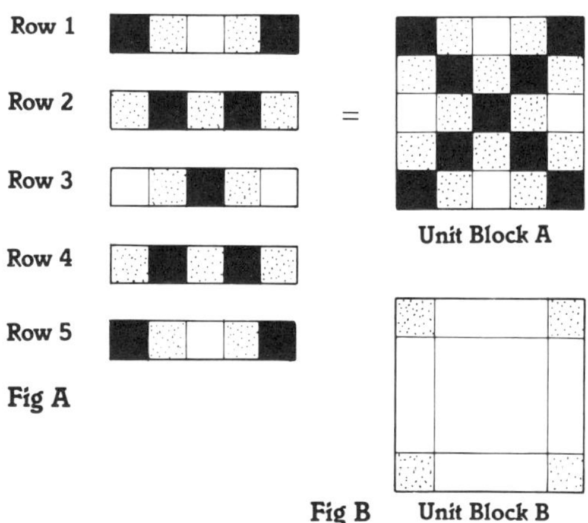

Fig A

Fig B

ANALYZE—FIND THE UNIT BLOCK

Since you can make the nine patch, you can make The Double Irish Chain. Just add two more rows of strips in both directions. You could call it a 25 patch, the technique is the same. The Double Irish Chain is a wonderful quilt because it is so recognizable, so versatile and so popular. It requires only three fabrics. Monochromatic light, medium and dark is the easiest combination (see Double Irish photos on back cover). The soft Glendale Gardens quilt is another example and has even less contrast. It features a printed border. If you have three fabrics that you like together, they can usually go in any of the positions.

The Double Irish Chain has two unit blocks. Block A is a square made of 25 squares, **Fig A**. Block B is a square of the same size with a small square in each corner, **Fig B**. Alternating the blocks develops the strong diagonal pattern. Unless you plan to do lots of hand quilting, don't put a solid color fabric in the Block B position. It will look so empty. Usually the Block B position has a light or medium colored fabric and darks and brights are used as accents in the chain design. That's certainly not a rule and there are beautiful quilts with dark fabrics in the Block B position as you can see in the color photographs on pages 22 and 24.

Rose and Muslin Double Irish Chain

Glendale Gardens Double Irish Chain

CUTTING AND SEWING

Unit Block A is a snap. Make a set of strips for every row, **Fig C**. Rows 1 and 5 are the same and rows 2 and 4 are the same. Press seams toward the dark fabrics. This is automatic pinning at its finest. Lay these sets of strips right sides together just like you did with the four patch and the nine patch. Then cut across the sewn strips the same width as the original strips. They are ready to be chain pieced. The pieced strip for row 3 is cut independently and added between rows 2 & 4. That particular step is the easiest place to make a mistake in this quilt. Make sure you are adding row 3 to the bottom of row 2 instead of the top of row 1.

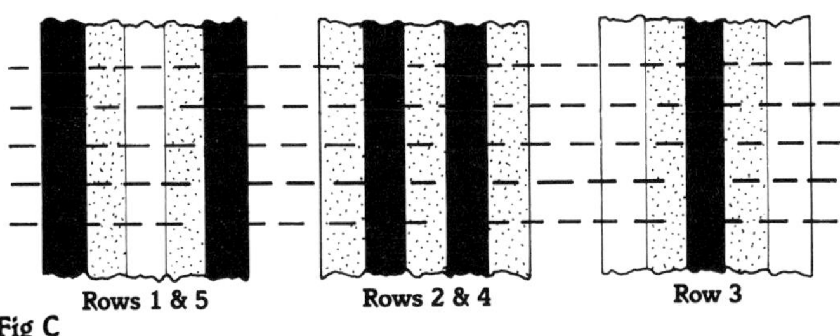

Fig C

Unit Block B is a square the same size as the finished Unit Block A, with small squares in the corners. Once again, make a row of strips for every row in the block. In this case there are three rows. Rows 1 and 3 are the same and are the same size as the rows in Unit Block A, **Fig D**. Row 2 is determined by the **finished** size of rows 2, 3 and 4 in Block A—again, actual measurement, not theory—plus ½". That is also the size of the middle strip in rows 1 and 3.

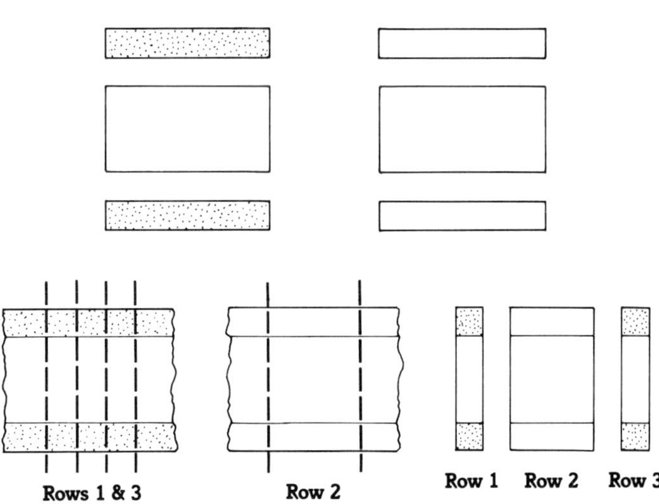

Fig D

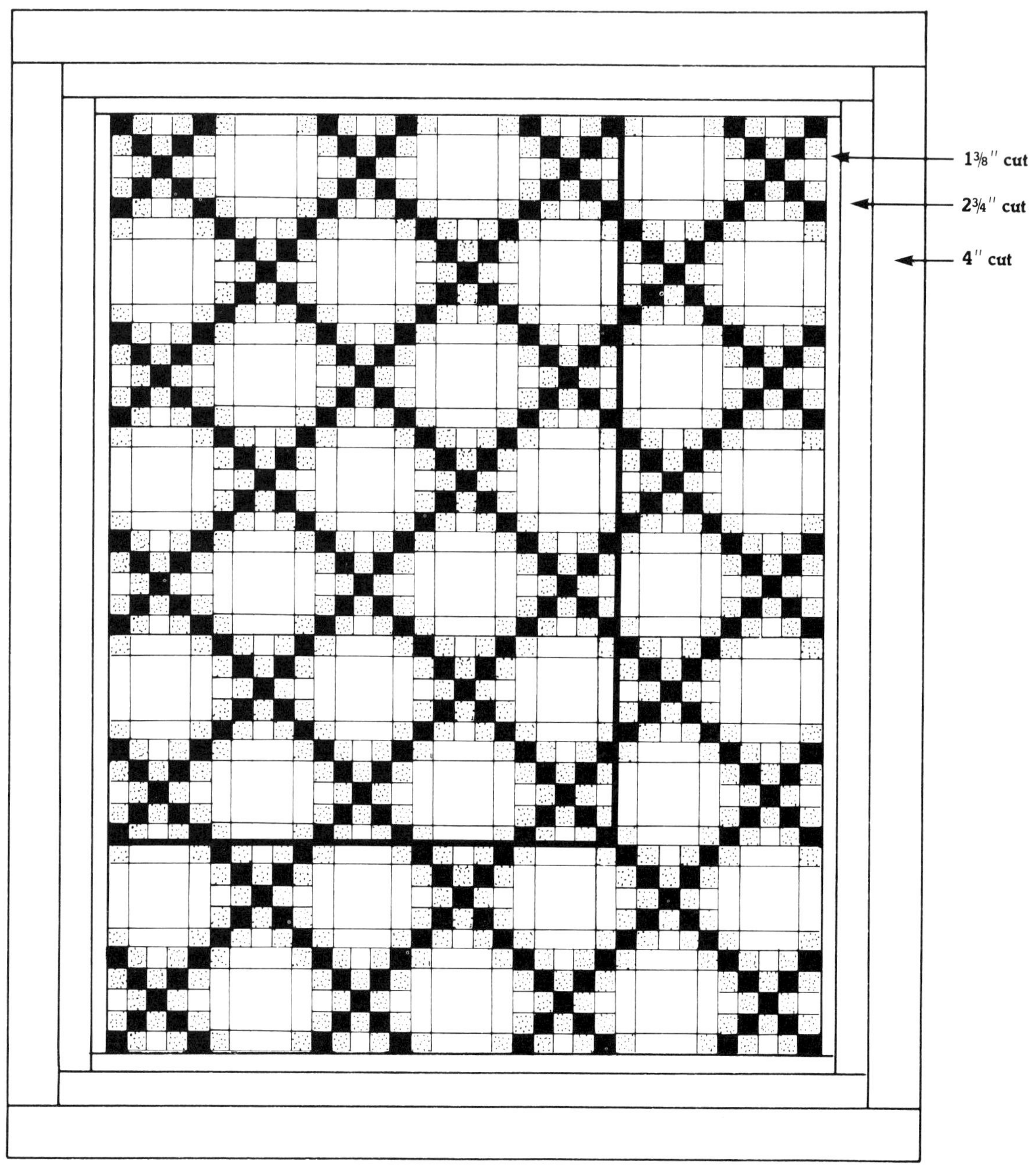

Fig E

Perhaps more interesting is the fact that in row 2, you are sewing strips of the same fabric together. Since there is a seam one row in on two sides of Unit Block B, it looks more balanced to have a seam on the other two sides. Also, for machine quilting, it makes a ditch to stitch in. If your family thinks you've gone off the deep end with patchwork, this particular step is good to do after everyone else is in bed. Some people shake their heads trying to figure out our enjoyment in cutting up contrasting fabrics and sewing them back together. They will really worry when the fabric matches.

Concentrate on organization when you work on Double Irish Chain. You will be well rewarded. It is an amazing quilt to produce quickly. Think smart and save time. When cutting strips, don't forget to put fabrics facing each other that will be facing each other in the first seam.

Like all quilts than can be drawn on a grid, the Double Irish Chain can be made with any size strips. Generally, the 2½″ cut strip used for the Rose and Muslin is my favorite for a Queen/Double quilt. The layout for that quilt, **Fig E**, shows that it is 7 blocks wide by 9 blocks high. The Glendale Gardens quilt uses a 3″ cut strip and therefore needs to be only 5 blocks wide by 7 blocks high to end up with the same size quilt as marked on **Fig E**. Obviously the 3″ strip will save you a lot of time. You will be making 28 fewer blocks!

The wall hanging size quilts are made with a 2″ cut strip, 5 blocks wide by 5 blocks high.

Double Irish Chain Wall Hangings or Tablecloths showing different placement of dark, medium and light fabrics

Burgoyne Surrounded

FABRIC REQUIREMENTS (45″-wide fabric)
For Burgoyne Surrounded, approximately 42¾″ square
(shown on page 39 and back cover)
⅜ yd Dark fabric
1½ yds Light fabric
⅜ yd Medium fabric
⅝ yd outside "border" fabric
Strips for smallest square: 1¼″ cut, ¾″ finished

ANALYZE—FIND THE UNIT BLOCK

When looking for the unit block in this quilt, it seems more accurate to say it has a master unit with many component unit blocks. The wall hanging shown is made of 9 master units. By changing the coloring of the outside strips, the illusion of separate borders was created.

CUTTING AND SEWING

Study the diagram and speed piecing diagrams for the wall hanging, **Figs A, B** and **C**.

You have seen that we start with the smallest strips to be pieced and then **make** subsequent pieces match the finished patchwork. In this quilt, the starting strip is a 1¼″ cut. The wall hanging is approximately 42¾″ square. It has over 1000 pieces, yet was completed in less than a work week. Remember that **Fig A** is a grid, and if you start with a strip cut 1¾″, your wall hanging would have a finished size of 71¾″ square.

The Burgoyne Surrounded pattern is ideal for practicing and perfecting machine piecing accuracy. There are many different shapes and different units. Inaccuracy will compound itself and really catch up with you in a project like this. One of the most helpful tips in your organization is to sew a pieced section to a non-pieced whenever possible. The non-pieced section usually has a newly cut straight edge that has the perfect ¼″ seam allowance.

Some people check and mark with a new template, and recut after nearly every piecing step. My philosophy is to learn how to adjust, compromise and judge so I won't have to do that. I want to eliminate the tedious whenever possible. However, the acrylic templates that have concentric squares marked on them make trimming irregular shapes with the rotary cutter and protective mat very quick and accurate. Some people mark the correct size of each finished unit on a muslin piece on the ironing board, and check for accuracy while pressing. Problem is, it's easy to cover marks and hard to make corrections.

Fig A

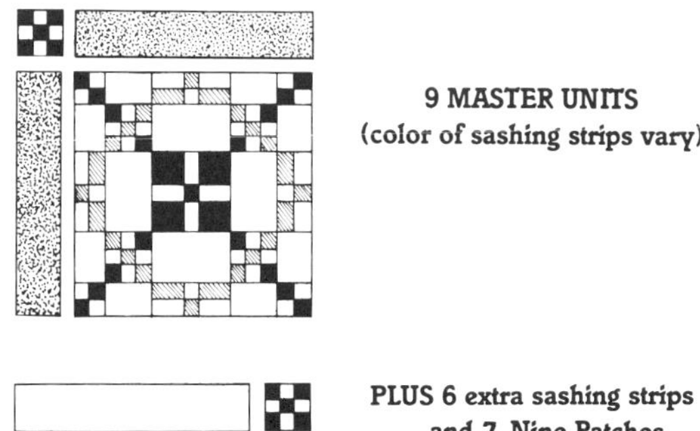

Fig B

Burgoyne Surrounded Wall Hanging

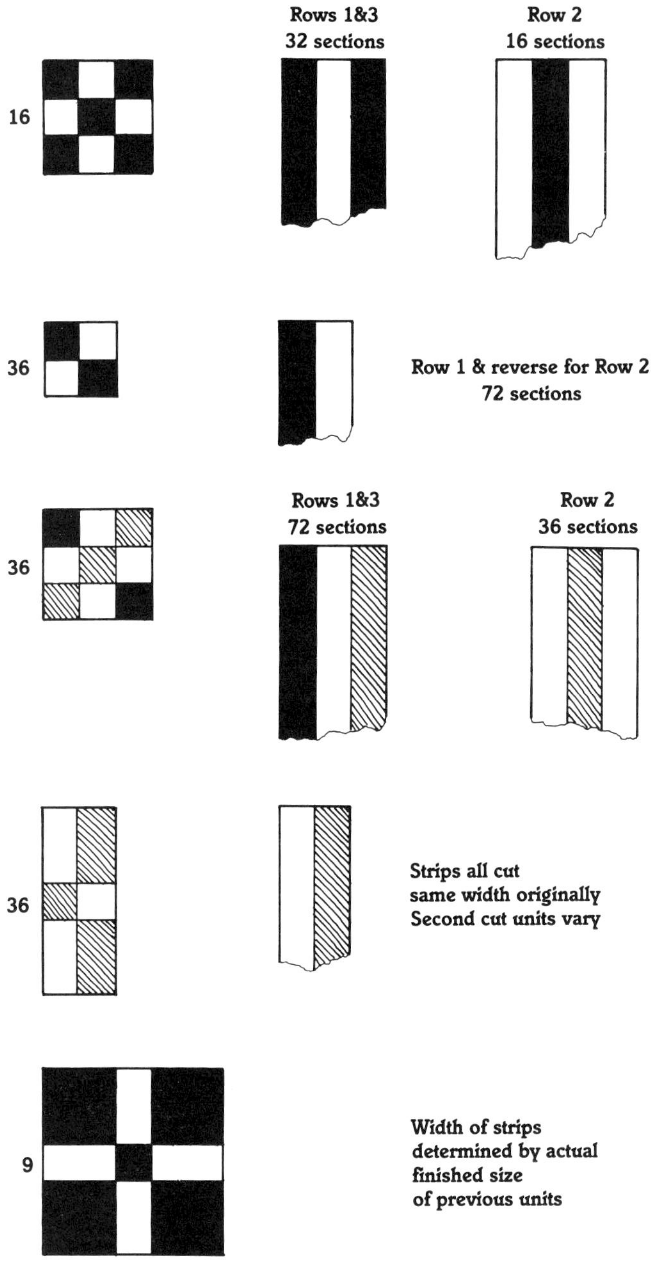

Fig C

PAPER VS. FABRIC

It's easy on paper to make all the pieces fit. Two 2″ squares will match one 4″ square. But fabric seems to have a mind of its own. Sometimes, even when we cut perfectly, a piece is slightly crooked during the sewing process or the stitching causes an edge to creep. At any rate, when you get ready for the next step, the sizes are not perfect. What to do? In the example above where two 2″ squares are to be joined to a 4″ square, center the seamed piece on the non-seamed and let both side seam allowances absorb part of the error.

Use your head to make adjustments as you go along. Use all the clues available. On straight line patchwork, the edge of the piece being stitched should be parallel to something! Find it, make sure the "throat plate" edge lines up, the width of pieces in chain piecing should be the same, etc. When you are visually insecure, use a ruler. It shouldn't be necessary very often, but I keep a small ruler at the machine to check the size of the exposed fabric.

Finishing Your Quilt

Only two of the many ways to finish a quilt will be discussed. They are tying and basic machine quilting. The method I use most is machine quilting "in the ditch" and binding with a separate, straight grain, double fold binding (finished with blunt corners, not mitered). When tying, the only difference is a tied center section instead of quilted. Usually, I add borders **quilt-as-you-sew.**

Tying the Quilt

If you are tying your quilt you will still prepare the layers and pin them as described in the following "Preparation for Machine Quilting" section.

Thread a 36" length of yarn into a large-eyed sharp-pointed needle. Double but don't knot! Working from center of the quilt out toward the edges, take needle down from the top through all three layers, leaving a tail of yarn long enough to tie. Bring needle back up from wrong side to right side, about 1/8" from where needle first entered. If tying at a seamed intersection, the seam allowance will make it necessary to take a larger stitch. Tie a square knot, then cut, leaving both ends about 1/2" long. To save time, you can take a few stitches at once, clip yarn halfway between the stitches, tie knots and trim ends.

Preparation for Machine Quilting

Why machine quilting?

I love hand quilting—both doing it and looking at it. Hand quilting aficionados and anyone who has completely hand quilted anything, have a great appreciation for the hours of work. The uninitiated, however, almost invariably look at a hand-quilted quilt, look at you and say "Did you do that by hand?" You beam "Yes", then simply cannot believe the next question. "Couldn't they invent a machine to do that?"

They have. It's a sewing machine. You can't, of course, use any machine to make a hand stitch. The sewing machine stitch doesn't look like the hand stitch either. Until you get within a few feet or sometimes inches of a quilt, what you see is not the stitching, but the shadow created by the quilting indention. The machine quilting actually gives a crisper indention.

While I love hand quilting, I love making quilt tops more. I've learned, there's little personal satisfaction in a pile of unquilted tops.

In the early years of the current quilt revival, machine quilting wouldn't have been considered, but many people are more realistic today. It will change your life to begin thinking about appropriate times to machine quilt. Remember, everything's a trade-off. Piecing and quilting by hand because it was once done that way and that is what you want to reproduce is fine. Doing it all by hand to make it a "real quilt" is not legitimate. Machine quilting is real. And machine-quilted antique quilts though less common, do exist. In fact, machine quilting may take more skill than hand quilting, but it is a different skill. It is also much faster.

It is commonly thought that while pioneer women quickly converted to piecing by machine, they were much more reluctant to quilt by machine. You see, the quilting bees really were among the most important social times. Quilting around the frame gave everyone a chance to hear the news, to gossip and to express themselves with other adult women. I believe that is why they usually pieced by machine—something traditionally done alone—to have more quilt tops faster, yet quilted by hand in groups to preserve their social time. Lucky the quilter, today, who has a group to quilt with around a large frame. It is still fun and therapeutic. Lucky the quilter who can be comfortable with machine quilting because that quilter will be more productive.

The quilts in this book are perfect for straight line machine quilting. Their straight design lines are easy to follow with machine stitching. In fact, these quilts practically beg to be machine quilted. While hand quilting can enhance any of the quilts, the overall graphic designs can stand alone without really missing the hand quilting.

Nearly everyone wonders if they need a fancy machine to do the quilting. I have successfully quilted with all kinds of machines from very simple to the most expensive. Check your machine's quilting I.Q. on scraps first. If you have any problem, or don't like the look of the stitch, the first thing to check is the pressure of the presser foot. Too much pressure can make an undesirable rippling effect. Nearly every machine has an even feed attachment available that helps move all layers through the machine at the same rate.

PREPARING THE BACKING FABRIC

Because I prefer a separate binding, my backings need to be about two inches bigger in all directions than the finished quilt top and that is more for convenience than necessity. If borders are to be added later in quilt-as-you-sew style, you will need to allow for finished widths of borders. (If you want to bind the edges by bringing the backing around to the front, the backing size needs to be larger.) On small crib or wall quilts it's usually not necessary to piece backings. The typical 45″ wide fabric is wide enough and you just cut it slightly longer than the quilt. 60″, 90″ and even 108″ wide fabrics are becoming more available to make unpieced backings for larger quilts. Some people try sheets for backings, but they are usually a tighter weave and most aren't 100% cotton. So, they could be considered an option for machine quilting, but they are definitely not recommended for hand quilting.

Usually a quilt back is made from one fabric with minimal piecing. Nothing says that has to be. In fact, I find more and more of my quilt backs incorporating some degree of patchwork, a trick that allows me to use up fabric from my reserves so I can buy new fabric for tops! We have shown the pieced back I did for the cover quilt above.

The most common pieced back is a single seam centered lengthwise, **Fig A**.

Sometimes it is advantageous to make crosswise seams, **Fig B**.

Fig A seam centered lengthwise

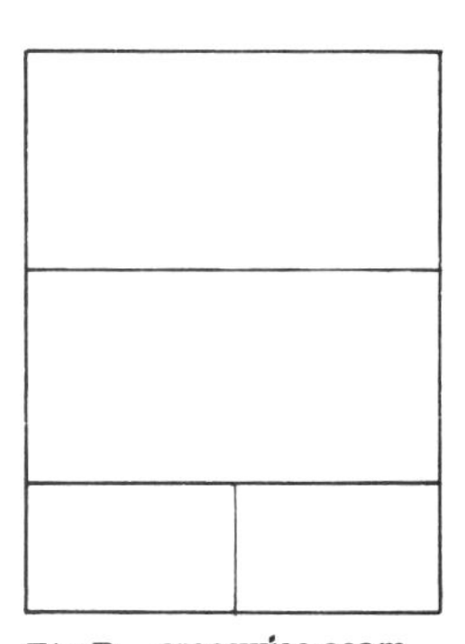

Fig B crosswise seam plus a pieced section

WHAT KIND OF BATTING

For machine quilting, my favorite batting is bonded polyester in a medium weight sometimes called all purpose.

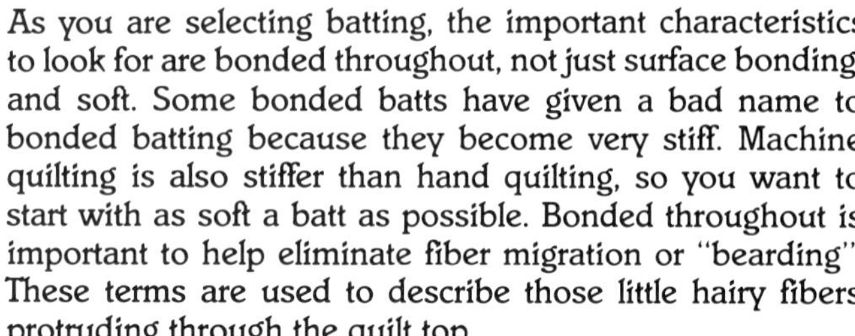

As you are selecting batting, the important characteristics to look for are bonded throughout, not just surface bonding, and soft. Some bonded batts have given a bad name to bonded batting because they become very stiff. Machine quilting is also stiffer than hand quilting, so you want to start with as soft a batt as possible. Bonded throughout is important to help eliminate fiber migration or "bearding". These terms are used to describe those little hairy fibers protruding through the quilt top.

There are typically three weights of batting available in the marketplace. They have different names, but generally speaking, there is the average weight batt used for most things. Low loft is used when you don't want much puff—usually used on garments and placemats, etc., and thick when you want extra loft.

Generally you want the all-purpose batting for machine quilting. Most people feel that the low loft does not add enough dimension to machine quilting. Thick batts are used when the end result you want is a comforter look. You might select that for tying, for example. If the batt is too thick, you may have to machine quilt in sections.

MACHINE QUILTING "IN THE DITCH"

Let's define "in the ditch", then we can quit putting it in quotes. "In the ditch" refers to stitching in the space created between two pieces of fabric that are sewn together.

"What space?", you say. Granted there isn't much, so you create a little more space by applying slight tension. Your fingers won't just walk, they'll pull away from the seam as the sewing machine feed dog pulls the fabric through the machine. That slight tension creates the extra space for stitching. When your fingers release the tension, the fabric returns to its natural position and tends to hide the stitching in the ditch.

MATERIALS NEEDED

At least one quilt top, batting and backing for layering. The backing should be pieced and pressed and the top pressed. Pay careful attention to the pressing and the direction of the seam allowances as you piece a quilt and this step will be easier. Check to make sure the quilt's opposite sides are the same length.

A table. Not just any table. A relatively long narrow table is best. The necessary size of the table depends on the quilt size, but at least five feet long for a double or queen quilt. Wall hangings and crib quilts could be done on a smaller table. It does not work on the ping pong table. It does not work on the floor or a round table or a king size bed. It's nice if the table has a center crack, but if it doesn't just measure and mark the center of both ends.

This table must not be a priceless antique, or even a pretty good one, because there is a great potential for scratching the surface of the table. You can put protective mats or cardboard cutting board on a table, but it will be better if you can find a firm surface.

A friend. You can layer a wall hanging alone, but for larger quilts, a friend makes it easier and more fun.

Two yardsticks or tape measures.

Safety pins. The minimum number for a queen/double quilt is about 350 pins. A crib quilt will use at least 75, etc. I like rustproof chrome plated #1 pins—they're about 3/4" long.

Invisible thread. Actually transparent is the word on most of the packages, but invisible sounds like more fun. It is a very fine nylon, not at all like the fishing line stuff available in the late 60's. It comes in clear and smoky. The smoky looks very dark on the spool, but one strand at a time, it's my favorite on everything but white and the lightest pastels. The clear reflects light on medium to dark fabrics.

Regular sewing machine thread for the bobbin that matches the backing fabric. Quilting thread is only for hand quilting.

THE ACTUAL LAYERING PROCESS

> After everything is gathered, the object is to center all three layers on themselves on the table.

Center the backing fabric on the table wrong side up. Center it both lengthwise and crosswise. Using a lengthwise center seam or marked center line in the backing fabric as the guide, line it up with the center of the table. Compare until you and your friend have the same number of inches hanging off each end.

Add the layer of batting in the same way. Smooth it out carefully. Remove packaged batting from the bag a day or two in advance so it can relax. A careful steam press can eliminate difficult humps and bumps. Make sure the batting completely covers the backing fabric.

Fold the quilt top in half right sides together and lay the fold on the center line. Make sure that equal lengths of fabric drop off the ends. When that is accurate, carefully open the quilt top. (If you must work alone, mark the center of the table on the quilt batt, fold the quilt top in quarters and place the double fold at the center point.) Open carefully.

Most quilt tops will be flat enough that you can just smooth them out. However, if you've had real problems piecing and the quilt top is very bumpy, you'll have to pat (in some cases pound) those bumps down. The fabric will scrunch up some in rough spots and you'll have to ease the top as you quilt, but it will look flat when you're through. If the bumps are really bad, you may have to shift to a fat batt! It truly will absorb the discrepancies better. The weight of the layers hanging off the table helps keep the fabrics smooth.

START PINNING

> How the quilt lays on the table, how it hangs and how you pin it will determine the position of all three layers when you quilt. Start in the middle and start pinning every four inches or in another selected pattern.

Think about your quilting plan now so that you avoid pinning where you want to stitch. One of the real benefits of pinning rather than basting, is that you don't put your hand under the quilt and move it out of position. Just pin from the top. When you feel the pin point touch the table top, pull it back up through the quilt and close. Basting is more disruptive and takes longer. Straight pins are not an alternative because they catch on the quilt and scratch you badly as you are working.

The number of pins per block or section depends on how many pins you have, how complicated the block is, etc. I recommend starting with more than you think you need and using less when you are more experienced.

Pin from the center out on the entire table surface. Pull the quilt to one side so that a new center section is on the table and work to one end. Everytime you move the quilt, double check to make sure you haven't developed wrinkles or folds in the backing fabric. When you have completed that half, go back to the center and start in the other direction.

NOW WHAT?

When you finish pinning, you are going to look at that quilt and say, "The part I still don't understand is how to get that great big quilt through the little opening in my sewing machine." That's right, the question is how do you stay in control instead of the quilt? The answer is by making it smaller and more manageable.

The first seam to quilt is the longest center seam. Everything to the right of that seam as you sit at the sewing machine must go through the arch. Starting at the edge, roll that side up to within four or five inches of the center seam. To the left of the seam, fold the quilt in nine or ten inch folds to the same distance from the seam, **Fig C.**

Now it's a long thin quilt. Starting at the end opposite where you will start sewing, roll the quilt up like a sleeping bag, **Fig D**. Suddenly you have a manageable quilt. Carry it to the machine.

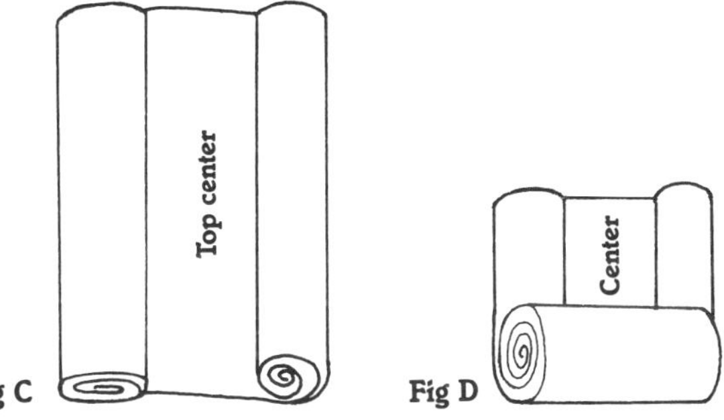

Fig C **Fig D**

SETTING UP THE MACHINE

Invisible nylon thread goes on the top only. Matching thread is okay on the top if low or no contrast fabrics are used. But if you have a dark red and ecru quilt and you are trying to stitch in the ditch with red thread, everywhere you miss and the red thread stitches on the ecru side, it is visible from 30 feet in moonlight, and vice versa.

While I like to use 10-12 stitches per inch for machine piecing, I change the stitch to 8-10 stitches per inch for quilting.

START QUILTING

Sit at the machine with the rolled quilt in your lap. Position the quilt so that the end of the seam you are quilting is under the needle. Lower the presser foot and start quilting. With both hands, pull away from the seam to make the ditch. You'll discover forgotten muscles in your shoulders. Stop and relax your back and shoulders between rows. Keep the quilt loose enough so that its weight doesn't pull against the needle. If your friend is there, you have a catcher. If not, you'll probably want a table in front of your sewing machine so the quilted section won't fall down and pull. When you have finished that seam, quilt the center horizontal seam. After that, I usually do two horizontal seams, one each side of center; then switch back to vertical, continuing to work out from center.

I hate to be the one to have to tell you, but you have to re-roll for every seam. Machine quilting goes in fast, but it isn't fast to take out. You want to stay in control of the quilt. As you re-roll, check the quilt back for newly sewn pleats. It's a personal decision, but I don't take out those little puckers, most often found at seam crossings. If there's a tuck you could catch your toe in, you have to correct it. In between is a gray area.

When you are all done, check the back again, check the front and trim any missed threads (I like to trim threads as I go so they don't get caught in other rows of stitching.) Remove the pins and get ready to add the borders or binding.

QUILT-AS-YOU-SEW BORDERS

The nice thing about adding borders using the quilt-as-you-sew technique, is that you are making a seam anyway, why not quilt at the same time? Measure and cut the quilt borders. Unless I have a design such as the floral border on the pink Double Irish Chain that demands mitering, I find crossed or blunt borders to be just fine. I like to add the side borders first and then the ends. When there are several borders, I usually add them one fabric at a time to create more quilting.

Put the quilt right side up on a large flat surface. Put the first side border right side down on top of the quilt just as if you were making a regular seam. Pin in place. Stitch through all thicknesses, quilting and seaming at the same time. Do the opposite side border. Open new borders flat into the proper position before adding borders on the ends of the quilt.

Proceed around the quilt in the same order for each border.

MAKING THE DOUBLE FOLD BINDING

MY FAVORITE BINDING IS CUT ON THE STRAIGHT, PREFERABLY UNSEAMED LENGTHWISE GRAIN AND FOLDED IN HALF. Bias is only necessary if the edge is curvy. Some people believe that bias will wear longer, but I don't have evidence to show that that outweighs the time to make bias, or even that it is a fact. My favorite width for binding is whatever I think will look best on that quilt. Some quilts look best with the tiniest 3/8" finished binding. Others need a 3/4" to 1" binding. Look at the quilt photographs to see how varied the decisions are.

My favorite binding is cut four times the desired finished width **PLUS** 1/2" for two seam allowances **AND** 1/8" to 1/4" to go around the thickness of the quilt. The fatter the batt the more you need to allow here. Fold and press binding strip in half (wrong sides together) so that the raw edges are even.

Usually I machine baste all the way around the quilt, 1/4" from the raw edge of the patchwork before trimming excess quilt batting and backing. Because I like full feeling bindings, I cut batting and backing that extends beyond the basting, almost but not quite twice as wide as the desired **finished** binding (**Fig E**). When the binding is stitched onto the quilt and pulled flat onto the batting (**Fig F**), it should be slightly wider than the batting.

Lay binding on quilt so that both raw edges of binding match the raw edge of the quilt top and stitch in place. Roll

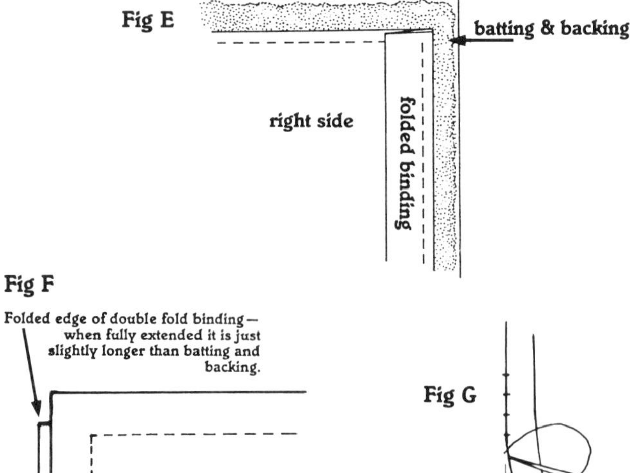

Fig F

Folded edge of double fold binding—when fully extended it is just slightly longer than batting and backing.

backing

Fig G

backing

double fold binding

binding around raw edge of quilt to the back (**Fig G**) and hand stitch in place using the row of machine stitching as a stabilizer and a guide. Add binding strips in the same order as borders.

To make blunt corners (I feel mitered corners aren't necessary on most simple borders), add bindings on sides of quilt first and complete the hand stitching. Measure quilt ends carefully. Add 1/2" at each binding end. To eliminate raw edges, turn that 1/2" back on the wrong side before stitching in place.

The hand hemming stitch I use is hidden. The needle comes out of the quilt and takes a bite of the binding and reenters the quilt exactly behind the stitch. The thread is carried in the layers of the quilt, not on the outside. At corners carefully stitch ends shut.